MW00803060

Literatures of the Americas

Series Editor
Norma E. Cantú
Trinity University
San Antonio, TX, USA

This series seeks to bring forth contemporary critical interventions within a hemispheric perspective, with an emphasis on perspectives from Latin America. Books in the series highlight work that explores concerns in literature in different cultural contexts across historical and geographical boundaries and also include work on the specific Latina/o realities in the United States. Designed to explore key questions confronting contemporary issues of literary and cultural import, *Literatures of the Americas* is rooted in traditional approaches to literary criticism but seeks to include cutting-edge scholarship using theories from postcolonial, critical race, and ecofeminist approaches.

More information about this series at
http://www.palgrave.com/gp/series/14819

Dominique Jullien

Borges, Buddhism and World Literature

A Morphology of Renunciation Tales

Dominique Jullien
Department of French and
  Italian, Comparative Literature
  Program
University of California, Santa Barbara
Santa Barbara, CA, USA

Literatures of the Americas
ISBN 978-3-030-04716-0   ISBN 978-3-030-04717-7   (eBook)
https://doi.org/10.1007/978-3-030-04717-7

Library of Congress Control Number: 2018964583

This Palgrave Macmillan imprint is published by the registered company Springer Nature
Switzerland AG
The registered company address is: Gewerbestrasse 11, 6330 Cham, Switzerland

Acknowledgements

I am happy to acknowledge the many people who have critiqued, advised, or simply encouraged me during the years of imagining, writing, and rewriting this book.

I received valuable feedback at numerous conferences where incremental bits of this book were first tried out. I am thankful to the students from S. Jill Levine's and Jorge Luis Castillo's Borges seminar at UCSB, where I gave a first overview of my project, and especially to my students from the Borges seminar I had the good fortune to teach in 2017 at the Harvard Institute for World Literature in Copenhagen. Their excellent questions and insights spurred me to rethink or reshape some of the arguments.

Over the years, I have benefited immeasurably from discussing various aspects of this project with wonderful colleagues and friends both far and near, whose careful listening and brilliant suggestions pushed me to sharpen the big picture or reframe ideas: Marco Bernini, Piero Boitani, Aboubakr Chraïbi, Souleymane Bachir Diagne, Paulo Lemos Horta, Stefan Helgesson, Vincent Kaufmann, Florence Klein, Françoise Lavocat, S. Jill Levine, Sandra Laugier, Florian Mussgnug, Hélène Mitjavile, Peter Madsen, Catherine Nesci, Sophie Niedergang, Francesca Orsini, Christopher Prendergast, Glyn Salton-Cox, Ram Seshadri, Christine Thomas, Galin Tihanov, Mads Rosendahl Thomsen, Marco Tavani, Delia Ungureanu, Marina Warner, and Kay Young—my thanks to all of them.

I gratefully acknowledge the anonymous Palgrave reader for incisive and stimulating criticism. I am especially indebted to the generosity of interlocutors who took time to read, or re-read, parts of the book-in-progress: Grégoire Halbout, Béatrice Baboulet, Efraín Kristal, Wen-chin Ouyang, and Sowon Park all shared their wisdom at various stages and helped the manuscript come to life. Their friendship, support, and continued interest in my work mean much to me.

Writing books is a solitary affair, but it happens in the home. To my family, I owe the largest debt of gratitude. Nina and Mamzelle gave their purring approval to many a page, while their habit of stretching over notes, books and keyboard redefined the notion of close reading. As always, my greatest thanks go to my daughters, who witnessed this other kind of birth pangs, and to my husband, who believes in me, even when I can't think why.

This book began with my curiosity about an enigmatic story of a king leaving his palace. I did not think it would relate to anything happening in the present. Since I began writing it, time has made that story, and the political anxiety at its source, painfully relevant once again.

PRAISE FOR *BORGES, BUDDHISM AND WORLD LITERATURE*

"When it comes to Jorge Luis Borges, the genius is in the details. In *Borges, Buddhism and World Literature*, Dominique Jullien carefully shows how this eponymous leitmotif permeates Borges' work and connects it to the world's literatures and to questions of philosophy, poetics and politics alike. With its refined sense of the concrete and its broad range of references that develop the many facets of the guiding theme, Professor Jullien's book is not to be missed by anyone with an interest in Borges."

—Mads Rosendahl Thomsen, *Aarhus University, Denmark*

"A king leaves his palace to become a monk, following a dialogue with an ascetic. This is the Great Renunciation scene found many times in stories around the world. Dominique Jullien's *Borges, Buddhism and World Literature* picks up Borges' lifelong attachment to Buddhism and examines his morphological model for the circulation of narrative. Touching on issues of politics and philosophy, the book presents a most original view of world literature, where the author analyzes Borges' own stories and then successfully tries the pattern to writers as diverse as amongst others Burton, Kipling, Kafka, Yourcenar, Blixen and Coetzee. A brilliant feat of criticism, and a thoroughly enjoyable read."

—Piero Boitani, *University of Rome 'La Sapienza' and University of Italian Switzerland*

"Jullien has written a seminal account of renunciation as a circulating narrative framework and a wider cultural gesture. She has managed to tease out its political and aesthetic implications in an extensive corpus of stories within and beyond the Borgesian hypertext. Students of world literature and Latin American culture will find this a very stimulating read."
—Galin Tihanov, *Queen Mary University of London, UK*

CONTENTS

Introduction: Leaving the Palace

Abstract The archetypal story of the king who leaves his palace to become an ascetic is introduced in the context of Argentine writer Jorge Luis Borges, who devoted several essays and a book to the most famous version of that renunciation story, the story of Buddha. The introduction explores Borges's lifelong interest in and knowledge of Buddhism, which relies heavily on nineteenth-century sources, many of these English, and weaves the main philosophical notions of Buddhist doctrine into a paradigmatically Borgesian triangle linking Buddhism, Schopenhauer, and Idealism. The story's political dimension sets up a recurring confrontation between power and powerlessness: it is connected to Borges's own predicament in Perón's Argentina, while the renunciation trope is connected to his personal ordeal as a writer losing his eyesight. The introduction also sets out to map how the renunciation story, as a traveling, adaptable and metamorphic story, allowed Borges to formulate a morphological model of narrative circulation that serves both as a reading principle (close to contemporary theories of world literature such as Damrosch's in particular) and a writing practice for his own texts. It lays the groundwork for the four main reading paths of this book on Borgesian renunciation stories: morphological, political, poetic, and parabolic.

Keywords Borges · Buddhism · Orientalism · Renunciation Morphology · Politics · Perón · Blindness · Introduction

> On another outing, the last, he sees a monk of the mendicant orders who desires neither to live nor to die. Peace is on his face; Siddharta has found the way. (Borges, "Forms of a Legend")[1]

> Tales have wings. (Richard Burton, *Terminal Essay*)[2]

A king, venturing beyond the palace walls, meets an ascetic, and decides to leave his palace, forsaking his life of power and luxury for one of asceticism and eventual enlightenment. This is the core of the Buddha legend, with a multitude of variations that either predate or postdate its appropriation as Buddhism's central and defining story. The story holds a special fascination for Jorge Luis Borges, whose interest in Buddhism was early and long-lasting. Borges wrote a cluster of essays that touch on Buddhism and the Great Renunciation episode during the 1950s, a time of great personal and political upheaval and a key transitional period marking a shift to a different literary style. These essays[3] sowed the seeds for Borges's later work on Buddhism (*What Is Buddhism?* written in collaboration with Alicia Jurado in 1976, along with "Buddhism", a long lecture published in *Seven Nights*, 1980). More importantly, they articulate a number of crucial paradigms that go to the heart of Borgesian poetics, and that open new paths of inquiry into world literature viewed in a Borgesian light.

The Great Renunciation is recalled in each essay, suggesting that it holds special significance for Borges.[4] A powerful story, it speaks to Borges on multiple levels—political, metaphysical, philosophical, literary. Renunciation stories are compelling, Geoffrey G. Harpham argues, because they manifest the universal "ascetic imperative", the transcultural impetus toward asceticism.[5] The story is also forceful politically: at its heart, we find a stark confrontation between power and powerlessness,

---

[1] *SNF* 374.

[2] Burton X: 120.

[3] The main essays examined here are collected in *SNF*: "Personality and the Buddha" (347–350), "Forms of a Legend" (373–376), and "The Dialogues of Ascetic and King" (382–385). Borges also added a reference to the iconic dialogue between king Milinda and the ascetic Nagasena to his earlier essay "A New Refutation of Time" (337–333) when he republished it in 1952, his Buddha period: Flynn 20. See also the later works *QB* (1976) and *SN* 58–75.

[4] Respectively *SNF* 348, 373–374, 384.

[5] Harpham 1987.

and when it is used, as often, in a didactic context, its aim is often the education of a king, relating it generically to the mirror for princes tradition. Furthermore, because the story of a king leaving his palace is highly adaptable, it is a traveling story, found in multiple variants, from the *Mahabharata* to the life of the Buddha, the Islamic legend of Bilawar and Budasaf, or the Christian legend of Barlaam and Josaphat. From a narrative standpoint, the story appeals to Borges because of its emphasis on plot over character: like Borges's life stories, it hinges on epiphany and destiny.

Sources of Borges's Buddhism

While the story is rooted in Buddhism, its significance and ramifications in Borges's aesthetics are obviously much broader. In order to assess Borges's take on Buddhism and the Renunciation story, it will be helpful to survey the scholarly sources that Borges drew on. These were instrumental in shaping key patterns and issues, among these Borges's focus on the story's transcultural mobility, which dovetails with his cosmopolitan view of literature.

Famously, Borges "grew up in a garden, behind a speared railing, and in a library of unlimited English books".[6] Like much of Borges's erudition, his knowledge of Buddhism is rooted in nineteenth-century European scholarship, much of it English. By his own account, he first encountered Buddhism in Edwin Arnold's best-selling poem *The Light of Asia*, which he read as a child in his father's library, and whose memory would accompany him for the rest of his life.[7] As many scholars have shown, a well-informed interest in Buddhism was not unusual among educated Victorian readers.[8] The essays written in the Fifties refer to major nineteenth-century scholars of Buddhism, in addition to key Buddhist treatises that were available to Borges in English translation.[9]

---

[6] Prologue to *Evaristo Carriego*, quoted in Rodríguez Monegal 3.

[7] Barili 50–51, Ferrari 217, San Francisco 147.

[8] P. Almond (1988: 32), Franklin 1–24, Wright 98–100.

[9] The essays show that Borges was familiar with some of the main Buddhist treatises, the fifth-century *Visuddhimagga* or *Path of Purity*, the first theological summa of Buddhism ("Personality and the Buddha", *SNF* 349), the *Yajur Veda* and the *Majjhima-nikaya* as well as the Sanskrit epic *Buddhacarita* and the legendary biography *Lalitavistara* ("Forms of a Legend", *SNF* 373, 375). A favorite reference, the *Milinda Pañha* in Rhys Davids's 1890–1894 translation included in Max Müller's multi-volume edition of the *Sacred Books of the East*, is mentioned twice ("Dialogues" *SNF* 383 and "Refutation", *SNF* 317).

The *Milinda Pañha*, "a novel of doctrinal intent composed in the north of India at the beginning of our era" (*SNF* 383) is mentioned twice: its argument (the story of a king who leaves his palace to become a buddhist monk, following a dialogue with an ascetic) gives it thematic prominence, as does the translator, T. W. Rhys Davids, the leading Pali scholar and authority on Theravada Buddhism among Victorian specialists. Rhys Davids also authored over 25 entries on Buddhism, including "Buddha", "Buddhism", and "Milinda", in the 1911 *Encyclopedia Britannica*, of Borgesian fame.[10] This shows that Borges was knowledgeable about both primary texts and secondary literature. It also anchors his erudition in the broader Victorian period.

The essay "Personality and the Buddha" lists no fewer than nine eminent Orientalist scholars from the turn of the century, including Edmund Hardy (*Der Buddhismus*, 1890), Karl Eugen Neumann (translator of the *Dhammapada* among other Pali canonical texts, 1893), Hermann Beckh (*Buddhismus: Buddha und seine Lehre*, 1916), Friedrich Zimmermann (*Buddhist Catechism*, 1888), Émile Senart (*Essai sur la légende du Buddha*, 1875), Jan Hendrik Kern (*History of Buddhism in India*, 1881–83; *Manual of Indian Buddhism* 1896), Otto Franke (*Geschichte des Chinesischen Reiches*, 1932–1952), and of course Hermann Oldenberg (*Buddha: Sein Leben, seine Lehre, seine Gemeinde*, 1881; English translation 1882).[11] In the same vein, "Forms of a Legend" references Karl Friedrich Köppen (*Die Religion des Buddha* 1857–59), Alfred Foucher (*L'Art gréco-bouddhique du Gandhara*, 1905), Léon Wieger (*Bouddhisme chinois, II: Les Vies chinoises du Bouddha*, 1913), and Moriz Winternitz (*Geschichte der indischen Literatur*, 1905–1922), in addition to Hardy and Beckh.[12] "The Dialogues of Ascetic and King" has its roots in Max Müller's monumental edition of the *Sacred Books of the East* (1879–1910), "the most ambitious and daring editorial projects of late Victorian scholarship",[13]

---

[10] On the 1911 *Britannica* as a key source of inspiration, see Christ 280–281.

[11] *SNF* 347–350. Borges does not always give the titles of the works consulted: listed here are the most likely references. Kern's 1896 *Manual of Indian Buddhism* is also listed in the bibliography of *QB*.

[12] In addition, for the appropriation of the Buddha legend into Christian lore, Borges refers to Menéndez y Pelayo's 1905 *Orígenes de la novela* (*SNF* 375).

[13] Molendijk 1.

for which T. W. Rhys Davids translated the *Milinda Pañha*, also mentioned in "A New Refutation of time". Twenty years later, when he
wrote *¿Qué es el budismo?* with Alicia Jurado, Borges updated the bibliography to include scholars such as D. T. Suzuki, Max Ladner, Edward
J. Thomas, or Edward Conze,[14] while still retaining several older works
by Kern, Foucher, or Oldenberg.[15] This reliance on nineteenth-century
Orientalists is striking. Literarily, it may account for two important features of the essays: their focus on comparative mythology and their interest in the legendary dimension of the Buddhist life story. Philosophically,
the Borgesian interpretation is indebted to questions that dominated the
Victorian reception of Buddhism, particularly the debates surrounding
the notions of Karma and Nirvana.

The fascination for Buddhism in Victorian England, blossoming
far beyond scholarly Orientalism into such international best sellers as
Arnold's 1879 *Light of Asia*,[16] and leading to a "cultural counter-invasion"
of the imperial center by Oriental ideas and values, has been exten-
sively documented.[17] Departing from earlier attitudes which regarded
Christianity as the only true faith and all other religions as heathen errors,
the new "religious egalitarianism"[18] characteristic of comparative religion, so evident in Max Müller's *Sacred Books of the East* and other nineteenth-century undertakings, was marked by recurrent comparisons
between Buddhism and other religions, most insistently Christianity.[19] The
Victorian "construction of Buddhism"[20] paved the way for the distinctive

---

[14] *QB* 80.

[15] Arguably, the 1976 book, as well as the lecture collected in *SN* (which according to
Jurado was the starting point for the book) continue the Victorian tradition of popularizing
lectures and publications that helped familiarize large portions of the literate public to simple discussions of the Buddhist doctrine (Wright 99–100).

[16] Arnold's poem itself was based on studies quoted in Borges's essays, in particular
Hardy and Müller: Wright 86.

[17] Franklin 7; also Caracciolo 30, P. Almond (1988: 330), Clausen (1973).

[18] Wright 69; also Molendijk 151–161.

[19] On the systematic underlining of parallels between Buddha and Jesus by scholars
and poets alike, see Wright 97; P. Almond (1988: 56–66); Clausen (1975: 3–6); Franklin
27–28. The comparison was the cause of both success and controversy for *The Light of
Asia: Britannica* (1911 II: 634); P. Almond (1988: 66). It is striking that Borges's
"Personality and the Buddha", published in 1950, still engages with the emblematic
"Victorian Jesus-vs-Buddha debate" (Franklin 27), if only to debunk it.

[20] Franklin 5.

Borgesian approach to metaphysical doctrines, which combined agnosticism with cross-cultural interest in various faiths and a propensity to
equalize and juxtapose them in his writings as "various intonations" of the
same metaphor (*SNF* 353).

Borges's reliance on nineteenth-century sources may also account
for the relative centrality of the "Nirvana debate" in his essays. As many
scholars have pointed out, the Victorian reception of Buddhist metaphysics was particularly troubled by two notions that seemed most inas-
similable to a Christian, and more specifically a Protestant worldview:
Karma (which was at odds with the belief in individual accountability)
and Nirvana (which conflicted with the belief in the soul's immortality).[21]
The raging "Nirvana debate" most often pitted two common (mis)inter-
pretations against each other: a nihilistic interpretation (Nirvana literally
meant extinction, a view expounded for example by Max Müller), against
a universalist interpretation of Nirvana as the soul's absorption into creation (Arnold's poem for example ended on such a pantheistic note).[22]
"The question of Nirvana continued over the years to be debated essentially in the same terms—either it was the cessation of all conscious existence, or it was absorption of the individual soul into a divine essence".[23]
Rhys Davids in the *Britannica* interpreted annihilation in a moral sense:
Nirvana was "the disappearance of that sinful, yearning, grasping condition of mind and heart which would otherwise, according to the great
mystery of Karma, be the cause of renewed individual existence".[24]

Borges seemed to fluctuate between the nihilistic and universalist views of Nirvana, at times conflating it with Emerson's Over-Soul
concept,[25] at times claiming the radical dissolution of soul, subject,
and consciousness into nothingness. He devoted an entire chapter of
¿Qué es el Budismo? to the "problem of Nirvana", attempting to distinguish the concept from its Hindu antecedents and its Western parallels

---

[21] Franklin 23; P. Almond (1988: 84–90).

[22] P. Almond (1988: 103–108); Franklin 43–45; Clausen (1975). Arnold's final vision—
the most famous line of the poem, so memorable for Borges—is closer to Hinduism than
Buddhism: "The dewdrop slips / Into the shining sea!" (Wright 92).

[23] Clausen (1975: 11).

[24] Quoted in Clausen (1975: 11–12).

[25] Christ 242.

(*QB* 44–47). Echoing the Victorian readers' unease, he criticized the concept of Karma as one of the weak points of Buddhism (*QB* 37) and generally appeared to find the Buddhist nothingness of self problematic rather than liberating.[26]

Furthermore, Borges's interpretation of Buddhism was in part filtered through another intertext: the philosophy of Schopenhauer, which Borges repeatedly hailed as foundational.[27] This of course was not unique: Schopenhauer's *Welt als Wille und Vorstellung* was a major bridge to and from Buddhism, and exchanges between Schopenhauer's philosophy and Orientalist scholarship went both ways.[28] Borges came to Buddhism through his adolescent discovery of Schopenhauer in Geneva, readings later consolidated by late-night philosophical discussions with one of his Argentine mentors, his father's friend (and self-professed "total idealist") Macedonio Fernández.[29] The strong autobiographical roots of what would become a lifelong scholarly interest are remarkable (in fact Borges's combined attraction for Buddhism and Schopenhauer appears woven into his youthful love for the music of the German language and the fond memories of the Geneva years),[30] as is the idiosyncratic philosophical triangle that brought together Schopenhauer, Buddhism, and Idealism. To Borges, the central philosophical tenet of Buddhism was the unreality of the self, a position that linked it both to Schopenhauer and to the earlier idealist systems of Hume and Berkeley. The nexus was formed early on and lasted Borges's entire life: the later book on Buddhism still references chapter 63 of *Die Welt*.[31]

For the purposes of the present discussion, the question of the accuracy of Borges's interpretations matters much less than the ways in which the Buddha triangle, pulling together Buddhism, Schopenhauer, and

---

[26] Flynn 101.

[27] Paoli 175.

[28] Some of the scholars mentioned in Borges's essays, such as Neumann and Zimmermann, came to Buddhism through Schopenhauer, whose writings were also influential in spreading the nihilistic interpretation of Nirvana in nineteenth-century European circles: Ryan 51–52; Baumann 39; Franklin 180–183.

[29] San Francisco 149, Paoli 176–178. Borges himself never considered himself a philosopher and acknowledged that he often discovered and engaged with philosophical and metaphysical systems through second-hand sources: Griffin in Williamson (2013: 5).

[30] Paoli 173, 178.

[31] *QB* 24; Paoli 196.

Idealism in a shared negation of the individual self, yielded a serviceable pattern to decades of Borgesian stories, poems, and essays. The philosophical idea of the "nothingness of personality", thematized in one of the earliest essays (1922: *SNF* 3), found recurrent expression throughout Borges's non-fiction ("A New Refutation of Time", "Personality and the Buddha", or the Flaubert essays: *SNF* 317, 347, 386, 390), fiction ("The Immortal" or "Shakespeare's Memory": *CF* 183, 508) and poetry ("Poem of the Gifts" or "The Exile": *SP* 95, 363). From the illusion of personality to the dream of history, Schopenhauer provided a philosophical backbone and—perhaps more importantly—a master trope for literary invention. In an essay on Nathaniel Hawthorne, Borges recalls an image from *Parerga und Paralipomena* comparing history to a kaleidoscope in which designs change but not the pieces of glass (*OC* 2: 57). The creative matrix generated by this idiosyncratic Buddha triangle is the focus of the present inquiry, which revisits the often-quoted quip about philosophy and metaphysics being branches of fantastic literature[32] in light of the Borgesian love affair with Buddhism.

The lifelong aftershock caused by Borges's encounter with Schopenhauer and its intersection with Buddhism has been well chronicled. Scholars have documented the formative influence on Borges's philosophical ideas, and also the repercussions on the fundamentals of his art, particularly regarding the paradoxes of identity and the *coincidentia oppositorum*.[33] To Christ's seminal analysis of the triangulation of Schopenhauerian idealism, proto-Nietzschean myth of eternal recurrence, and Berkeleyan idealism as the foundational pattern in Borges's personal mythology, one should add Buddhism (filtered through its late nineteenth-century Western interpretation): it afforded the unifying background to these different intersecting theories.

The Shape of This Book

This book, while nourished by studies of the philosophico-metaphysical aspects of Borges's work,[34] has a different focus altogether. (For the same reason, I only touch briefly upon another important topic,

---

[32] Most explicitly in "Tlön, Uqbar, Orbis Tertius", *CF* 74; see Paoli 175.

[33] San Francisco 147–149; Paoli 196–198; Christ 18–34, especially 26–29.

[34] Bossart's fifth chapter is especially helpful if one wants to measure Borges's knowledge of Buddhism against other contemporary Western exponents of it, such as E. Conze.

which would no doubt deserve a study of its own: the later evolution of Borges's interest in Buddhism, inflected on a personal level by his discovery of Zen and Shintoism, Japanese culture, *haiku* and his relationship with María Kodama.)[35] My primary concern is neither with the doctrinal content (still less the accuracy) of Borges's knowledge of Buddhism, nor with the extent of his debt to various Orientalist scholars from the nineteenth century on. Rather, I look at the Buddhist material as a source of narrative inspiration. For instance, Borges repeatedly professed admiration for Buddhism as a tolerant, non-dogmatic religion that did not require faith in individual events and characters and allowed for agnosticism (*QB* 50, *SN* 58–59). This was both a philosophical position (and one that also had nineteenth-century roots)[36] and—more importantly for this book's perspective—an aesthetic position, which dispensed with the need for a historical approach and freed the poet to engage with the legend. In Borges's reworking, the Great Renunciation becomes the major turning point, just as it was in Arnold's beloved poem *The Light of Asia*. Arnold greatly expanded the incident, developing its dramatic and sentimental potential and memorializing it in his poem's subtitle: no doubt this particular slant contributed greatly to the poem's phenomenal success.[37] For Borges too the episode was foundational. This book focuses on the ways in which Borges wove the story of the Great Renunciation into a complex tapestry of interconnected narratives.

Viewing the Buddha as an archetype rather than a historical individual opened the way to thinking about the Buddha's story, in particular the climactic Renunciation episode, as legendary, with a focus on its variations and retellings. This too is a trait Borges shared with nineteenth-century scholars. Comparative mythology was keenly attentive to the ways in which legend and history intermingled (Rhys Davids's entry on "Buddha" in the 1911 *Britannica* stressed the layers of mythical accretions over the historical substratum)[38] as well as the ways in which stories

---

[35] On Borges's journey to Japan in 1979, see Williamson (2004: 441–446).

[36] See Borges's statement of his "essential skepticism" in 1952 epilogue to *Otras inquisiciones: OC* 2: 153. On the attractiveness of Buddhist tolerance, see P. Almond (1988: 128); Wright 97.

[37] Wright 87; San Francisco 155.

[38] Rhys Davids (1911: 4, 737).

traveled. "Tales have wings and fly farther than the jade hatchets of pro-to-historic days", wrote Richard Burton, the *Arabian Nights* translator admired by Borges.[39] The meanderings of tales across languages, cul-tures, and religions were traced by numerous scholars, and many such stories-about-a-story could provide inspiration to Borges: from the (unsigned) entry on Barlaam and Josaphat in the 1911 *Britannica*, to G. H. Gerould's 1905 survey of hagiological borrowings (which encom-passed Hindu epics, the *1001 Nights* and lives of the Christian hermits), Menéndez y Pelayo's 1905 *Orígenes de la novela* (which retraced the steps of Buddha into Christian lore) or Menéndez Pidal's 1902 essay (which tracked the circuitous route of the Buddha legend into the Spanish Golden Age theater, uncovering a proto-Borgesian link between Buddhism and the iconic Baroque theme of life-as-a-dream).[40]

Especially noteworthy are studies that highlight the splicing and over-lapping of different strands or segments of a legend. Rhys Davids noted that the Buddha legend resulted from the merging of the two Indian ideals of the Wise Man and the Golden Age King.[41] Obviously this was not lost on Borges, whose meditation on the archetypal dialogues of kings and ascetics is the starting point for these pages. More generally, nineteenth-century comparative mythology produced a constellation of studies detailing the cross-cultural migration of stories and highlighting the recurrent patterns beneath the variegated versions. Borges, I believe, expanded on this nineteenth-century tradition with his intuition of litera-ture as "morphology", a notion borrowed from Goethe's biological writ-ings and applied to literature. The transfer of the morphological model from the natural world to the world of art facilitated a Borgesian image of literature as potentially infinite variations on archetypal patterns.[42] The "legend" of the Great Renunciation—the climax of the Buddha story—serves as an entry point into Borges's morphological view of literature.

---

[39] Burton X: 120. More on Burton in Chapter 2.

[40] "Barlaam and Josaphat", *Britannica* (1911: 3, 403–404); Menéndez Pidal 6–56; Gerould 529–545. Menéndez y Pelayo's book is mentioned in *SNF* 375. For contempo-rary views of the "Christian Buddha", see P. Almond (1987: 391–406), as well as Lopez and McCracken's remarkable study (2014); however, they do not cite Spanish sources, which were easily available to Borges.

[41] Rhys Davids (1903: 11–12); also P. Almond (1988: 128).

[42] Borges's engagement with Goethe's morphology is discussed at greater length in Chapter 1.

The legendary paradigm appears foundational, first, as the antithesis of the realist novel: instead of the dominant fictional model predicated on length, materialism, and psychology, it allowed Borges to espouse a counter-model unfettered by historical facts and individual particulars. With its roots in the Buddhist negation of personality, the Renunciation legend also offered a narrative template free from psychology, whether of characters or of authors, according with and providing a configuration for the central Borgesian tenet of authorial anonymity. Last but not least, the legendary model also afforded an idiosyncratic solution to the challenges Borges faced after the 1950s, when his blindness became nearly complete: it allowed for a semi-oral compositional model, shifting the emphasis from individual writing to an intermediary form based on memory, shared authorship, retelling and retransmission.

Borges's essays on Buddhism, then, stand at the center of a rich nexus, bridging a lifelong interest in a religion felt to be in many ways congenial, and a view of literature that highlights the anonymity, mobility, and generative transformation of an archetypal pattern. His creative speculations on the Renunciation paradigm present a unique case of contemporary reinvention of a nineteenth-century Orientalist tradition. To a contemporary reader, they appear at first unquestionably "Orientalist" in the Saidian sense of the word, not only because of the sources on which they rely, but also because of the way in which the cycle of pattern-and-variation folds all of world literature into the topos of the timeless Orient.[43] Yet they also profoundly destabilize the traditional centripetal model of Western Orientalism. Perhaps, as Ian Almond has argued within the context of Islam, Borges's position is best understood as that of a "post-Orientalist", a writer whose "Islamic/Arabian stories uncritically draw on a tried and tested stock of familiar Orientalisms", but who nonetheless ends up rising above them through "a final realization of the fictitious foundations and illusory claims of the Orientalist project".[44] In fact, the relevance of Borges to postcolonial criticism has been coming into ever sharper focus. Robin Fiddian recently claimed that, if read properly, Borges is "a no less important figure [than Edward Said] in the history of colonial and postcolonial

---

[43] On the Orientalist fixation on timelessness and anti-modernism, see Makdisi 11.
[44] I. Almond (2004: 451).

discourse".[45] What seems clear is that Borges's dialogue with Eastern philosophy and Renunciation narratives, undertaken "from the edge of the West"[46] and from a culture entangled in its own postcolonial negotiations, hardly fits the Orientalist model originally described by Said and critically established in the wake of his ground-breaking book. Instead, as I hope to show, the multiplicity and mobility of references Borges accumulates in his writings on the Renunciation story sets in creative motion the very postulate of a fixed Western center on which Orientalism relies. Reimagined by a writer uniquely positioned at the margins of both East and West (seminally described in Sarlo's analysis)[47]—by the proverbial "Argentine adrift on a sea of metaphysics" (*SNF* 317)—the paradigm no longer follows a simple one-directional movement from East to West, but rather becomes multidirectional, envisioning stories that branch off one another in a potentially infinite maze-like shape.

Because Borges acknowledges the various levels on which the archetypal pattern of the king leaving his palace exerts its pull on our imagination, and because he articulates a key feature of the story (its adaptability and metamorphic nature), this book's thesis takes the Borgesian corpus as its anchor. However, the inquiry also extends beyond Borges, to a larger constellation of texts across world literature, in which the king and the ascetic are set up as mutual mirror images. Borges's morphological conception of literature suggests a strategy for reading other texts from the wider Borgesian hypertext—whether they are linked to Borges by the bonds of traditional influence, or the retrospective "correlation" of the "precursor" in the Borgesian sense (*SNF* 365). Hence this book proposes a double "act of reading"[48]: weaving in and out of Borges, it offers both a reading of the Borgesian corpus through the morphological lens, and a reading of the Renunciation story in a Borgesian network of tales.

The story of a king leaving his palace provides the starting point to four interconnected reading paths. Chapter 1, "*Renunciation, Morphology and World Literature*", draws primarily on Borges's essays on Buddhism written in the Fifties, setting up the Borgesian paradigm for Renunciation stories, and more generally views of Buddhism, as linked

---

[45] Fiddian 4.
[46] Sarlo 5.
[47] Sarlo 2–6.
[48] Manguel 25.

to a theory of literature as "morphology", that is, as a process of transformative plot generation. The "morphological" model of world literature intuited here is indicative of the resurgence of critical interest in
Goethe's *Weltliteratur* by Formalists in the 1920s, then by Structuralists
in the 1950s. It also dovetails with the influential postwar discussion of
Goethe's views by Fritz Strich. Whether this results from direct knowledge of literary theory, or a more diffuse meeting of minds,[49] Borges's
morphological speculations clearly interface with major critical devel-
opments. While scholars have analyzed Borges's ties to Structuralism
(J. Alazraki), his debt to Mircea Eliade's theory of archetypes
(R. Christ), his affinities with the Proppian homologies of folktale motifs
(M. Lusky Friedman) or mythic narrative patterning (C. Wheelock,
R. K. Britton),[50] revisiting these historical discussions through the lens
of the Renunciation story reveals the contemporary relevance of Borges's
morphology. Borges's intuition of literary morphology—seen through
the metamorphic Renunciation story generating an expansive network
of global texts—anticipates more recent (and more reader-centric)
theories of world literature that modernize, globalize and decenter the
old Goethean model, such as David Damrosch's definition of world
literature as a mode of circulation and of reading, or Wai Chee Dimock's
centrifugal theory.[51]

Alongside the theoretical and aesthetic questions raised by Borges's
morphological conception of literature, the theme of removal from
politics also assumed a new urgency, both ethically and politically: a
heightened significance attached to the figure of Buddha as Renouncer
in the context of Argentina's postwar political history. The first chapter
also takes stock of the basic tension between the political and apolitical
stance at the heart of the Renunciation story, whose powerful political resonance is one reason for its endurance and its ability to capture
imagination. In an apparent paradox, the story of political withdrawal
carries political efficiency. The second chapter, *"A Lesson for the King:
Renunciation and Politics"*, follows the political thread that runs through
the story, interrogating its purpose as a didactic story in a political context. Renunciation stories are told to kings in an attempt to control or

---

[49] Alazraki (1990: 104).

[50] Alazraki 104–107; Christ 33–35; Friedman 1–54; Wheelock 105–108; Britton
608–609.

[51] Damrosch 3–5; Dimock (2001: 174–178).

mitigate their tyrannical behavior. The king-and-ascetic dialogue sets up a confrontation between power and authority, which paradoxically the king loses to a powerless adversary. Chapter 2 explores this paradox, and the ways in which variants of renunciation stories can be used to achieve political goals, with renouncer figures serving as instruments of awareness in political genres—fables or mirrors for princes. The discussion reaches beyond Borges to a constellation of stories from the Borgesian hypertext (from Burton's hermit trilogy in the *1001 Nights* to Victorian renouncer stories) that complicate the pen-vs-sword problem. Ultimately, renunciation stories raise the bigger questions of the power of storytelling and the possibility of truth-telling that were central preoccupations for contemporary thinkers such as Hannah Arendt and Michel Foucault: the discussion goes from 'why would a king become an ascetic?' to 'what makes ascetics good narrative devices in a parrhesiastic situation?' It also attempts to reassess Borges's ambiguous take on this rich political tradition.

Chapter 3, *"From Ascetic to Poet: Poetic Renunciation"*, analyzes the morphological transformations of the renunciation archetype into a poetic or self-reflective narrative. In Borges's poet stories, the king-and-ascetic pair morphs into a king-and-poet pair, with renunciation serving an artistic goal: the discussion centers on the aesthetic variant of the renunciation paradigm. Ross Posnock's generous catalogue of aesthetic ascetics from the nineteenth century onwards, *Renunciation: Acts of Abandonment by Writers, Philosophers, and Artists* (2016), is an important interlocutor here. However, my discussion takes matters further back, tracing the aesthetic appropriation back to the Ancient and Renaissance tradition of artists' lives, and exploring sacrificial conceptions of art from Romanticism and Symbolism to the present. The analysis centers on the aesthetic asceticism of Borges's poet stories, alongside renunciant artist stories from the Borgesian hypertext (by Flaubert, Schwob, Yourcenar and Yi Mun-yol) where renunciation is a requirement of the creative process. The exploration of aesthetic asceticism also interfaces with the absorption of Cynic values into aesthetic ideals: Foucault's late work on Cynicism (especially his fruitful intuition about modern art's debt to cynicism),[52] and more generally the confluence

---

[52] For this reason, my analysis also travels along part of the same road as A. Rose's *Literary Cynics* (2017), although Rose makes no mention of the Buddhist legend undergirding the renunciation paradigm in Borges.

between Borges, Flaubert, Foucault, and Schwob are an essential backdrop to this chapter on renunciant artist characters.

Chapter 4, "*Modernity's Enigmatic Parables of Renunciation*", frames the story of the king leaving the palace within the broader question of modern parables, which appeal to and yet also frustrate readers' longing for exemplarity or revelation. The laws of circulation and incessant transformation that govern the archetypal Renunciation story take it to a breaking point, where its straightforward efficiency is lost, along with its spiritual or political agency. This is the situation of post-Kafka parables, which play out the loss of certain meaning. My final chapter engages with the enigmatic nature of the parable-like variants on the Renunciation story, both in Borges and beyond, in Kafka and Blixen. Major interlocutors here are contemporary parable critics, who follow in the footsteps of Walter Benjamin's ironic assessment of a post-transcendent genre. Like Kafka's enigmatic parables, modern stories of kings leaving the palace exert their persistent yet perplexing gravitational pull on the reader.

From Kipling's ascetics to Oscar Wilde's Happy Prince, from the Yellow Emperor to Persian princes in disguise, aristocratic Korean beggars, hermit shepherds, wandering Chinese painters, or saintly cynics: these are some of the characters that walk through these pages. They are characters, not concepts: "I think of all poetic theories as being mere tools for the writing of a poem", Borges claimed in *This Craft of verse* (*CV* 97). This book parses the ways in which Borges drew upon Buddhist matter as "a springboard for his fiction".[53] What captivates about kings becoming ascetics? The story possesses the appeal of paradox, certainly—it is a story that unsettles the polarized terms of king and ascetic, sets them in creative interplay, upends the fixed order of power, throws everything into circulation. The story of a wandering king is a story that wanders, that knows no boundaries. "From now on I have no kingdom, or my kingdom is limitless" (*SNF* 384): the "dizzying words" of a king abandoning a position of centrality for the margins might also apply to Borges's proto-cynical cosmopolitan aesthetics.

---

[53] Griffin in Williamson (2013: 11).

CHAPTER 1

A Borgesian Morphology: Renunciation, Morphology, and World Literature

Abstract Drawing primarily on Borges's essays on Buddhism written in the critical decade of the Fifties, this chapter sets up the Borgesian paradigm for Renunciation stories. Borges emphasizes their transcultural and transhistorical circulation—an idea that interfaces with his anti-nationalist aesthetics in "The Argentine Writer and Tradition"—and suggests a theory of literature as "morphology" (a notion borrowed from Goethe): a potentially infinite number of poems and stories generated by transformation of a finite number of "archetypes". Alongside this morphological conception of literature, the theme of apolitical withdrawal and the figure of Buddha as Renouncer also assume a heightened significance in the context of Argentina's postwar political history.

Keywords Buddha · Renunciation · Goethe · Morphology · Archetype · Circulation

Fate is partial to repetitions, variations, symmetries. ("The Plot")[1]

Infinite stories, infinitely branching. ("An Examination of the Works of Herbert Quain")[2]

[1] *The Maker, CF* 307.
[2] *Fictions, CF* 110.

© The Author(s) 2019   1
D. Jullien, *Borges, Buddhism and World Literature*, Literatures
of the Americas, https://doi.org/10.1007/978-3-030-04717-7_1

Borges's essays on Buddhism are contemporaneous with one of his most important essays, "The Argentine Writer and Tradition", a spirited defense of literary cosmopolitanism. The coincidence in time points to intersecting preoccupations in Borges's intellectual life. Why Buddhism? The legend of Siddharta who left his palace for a life of asceticism, a story that Borges repeated in each of his essays (as well as subsequent lectures and interviews on Buddhism), held aesthetic appeal as a "traveling" story—adapted and transformed into multiple cultural, linguistic, and religious contexts—at a time when Borges was forcefully rearticulating his position on the universality of literature. One essay alludes to Goethe's "morphology" (the study of the evolution of forms, driven by the intuition of the unity of all living forms), a model which accounts for both archetypal unity and dynamic transformation, in nature and in art. This allusion remained unelaborated: Borges never devoted a full-fledged essay to Goethe's morphological theory. Nevertheless, the affinities with his own views of literature as infinite transformations of a finite number of fundamental forms seem unmistakable, as well as the resonances with his own "decidedly monotonous" practice of literature.[3] The Buddhist Renunciation story provides a good case study for Borges's quasi "Goethean" intuition of literature as transformation and circulation of archetypes, and more generally invites comparison of Borges's literary universality with Goethe's *Weltliteratur*. The story's metaphysical appeal (particularly the denial of individualism) is no less important, as impersonality was a prominent Borgesian theme from the beginning ("The Nothingness of Personality" was first published in 1922). Ultimately, the Buddhist Renunciation legend also held a powerful existential appeal for Borges, particularly in the fifties: the story of a king leaving the palace, retold in multiple variants, suggests an underlying anxiety common to all Borges's writing at a politically fraught time which was also a major turning point in his life, when his blindness became nearly complete. The infinitely metamorphic Buddhist story lends itself to a meditation on the ways in which the accidents of life transform literature, and are transformed by literature in return. By following the thread of universal circulation and transformation that runs through the essays on Argentine

---

[3] "A mere handful of arguments have haunted me all these years; I am decidedly monotonous" (Foreword to *Brodie's Report*, *CF* 346).

literature and on Buddhism, as well as several fictions that can be read as transformations of a narrative type, this study reveals the Renunciation story at the heart of Buddhism as an exemplary nexus of key Borgesian interrogations on the reading and writing self.

1   A BORGESIAN MORPHOLOGY

1.1   *"The Universe Is Our Birthright": Buddhism and the Cosmopolitan Ideal*

In a strong statement against literary nationalism ("The Argentine Writer and Tradition", given as a lecture in 1951), Borges unambiguously claimed that Argentines should embrace cosmopolitanism: "I believe that our tradition is the whole of Western culture (...) we must believe that the universe is our birthright and try out every subject" (*SNF* 426–427).[4] This attraction toward the foreign was perhaps not unexpected coming from a bilingual intellectual who had grown up in a multicultural environment—Borges was part English on his father's side; he had spent vitally formative years in Switzerland, England and Spain, becoming fluent in French and German and even publishing his first poems in French.[5]

But "The Argentine Writer and Tradition" does not just advocate transcending national themes. It makes a far more ambitious claim: free circulation of literary themes and images is a prerequisite of national innovation. Borges ironically exposes the paradoxes of the quarrel: it would be unimaginable to deny Racine "the title of French poet for having sought out Greek and Latin subjects", or Shakespeare the right "to write *Hamlet*, with its Scandinavian subject matter": indeed "The Argentine cult of local color is a recent European cult that nationalists should reject as a foreign import". The camel paradox reinforces this point. The Koran does not mention camels, because it is an authentic

---

[4]Waisman 237 traces the complicated editorial history of the essay to argue for its centrality to Borges's aesthetics.

[5]On Borges's early writings in French and English, see Berveiller 75 and Williamson (2004: 59). On the bilingualism of the Borges household, see Rodríguez Monegal 15. Other discussions of Borges's cosmopolitan background and universalist views of literature include Sarlo 1–10, Balderston (1998: 37–48), Siskind (2007: 75–92), among others.

Arab book in no need of local color: likewise, Argentines should "believe in the possibility of being Argentine without abounding in local color" (*SNF* 423–424).[6]

The universal circulation of literary themes, so forcefully articulated in the 1951 lecture, is also thematized by the diversity of topics covered in the essays: Flaubert, Homer's translators, the poetry of tango, Walt Whitman, the Kabbalah, the *kenningar*, the *Thousand and One Nights*, and much more. In addition, Borges's fictions from beginning (*A Universal History of Infamy*) to end (*Shakespeare's Memory*) illustrate the principle of the circulation of stories across cultural spheres, typically by providing variations on a single basic plot. One such basic plot, the story of a king who leaves his palace to become a beggar—the Buddha legend—recurs throughout Borges's work in various avatars: it provides a good case study for the paradigm of transcultural appropriation and circulation.

1.2   *Borges's Essays on Buddhism, Narrative Circulation, and Morphology*

Borges's lifelong interest in Buddhism crystallized in the fifties in a cluster of essays ("Forms of a Legend", "The Dialogues of Ascetic and King", "Personality and the Buddha"), followed by the 1976 book coauthored with Alicia Jurado (*QB*), and lectures, interviews, and conversations where many of the same paradigms recur.[7] His engagement with the renunciation motif (which is mentioned in each one of the three essays and also features, with multiple variants, in Borges's fictions, particularly in parable form),[8] is integral to his view of literature as variations on archetypes and as a network of circulation.

In "Forms of a Legend" (1952) Borges tells the Renunciation story in some detail, highlighting the key moments of Siddharta's life: "the

---

[6]The 'camel paradox' which Borges found in Gibbon, is based on a factual error: I. Almond (2004: 441).

[7]"Buddhism", *SN* 58–75, *QB*, Borges et al. (2005, 2011).

[8]Especially "The Two Kings and the Two Labyrinths", *The Aleph* (*CF* 263–264), "Parable of the Palace", *The Maker* (*CF* 317–318), "The Mirror and the Mask", *The Book of Sand* (*CF* 451–454). The renunciation story's links to the parable is discussed in Chapter 4.

29 years of illusory happiness (...) dedicated to sensual pleasures", during which the young prince lived behind the palace walls, sheltered from the pain of the world on his father's orders, and the four life-changing discoveries *extra muros*: old age, disease, death, and finally the peaceful life of the ascetic which determined him, likewise, to renounce the luxury of his palace. "On another outing, the last, he sees a monk of the mendicant orders who desires neither to live nor to die. Peace is on his face; Siddharta has found the way" (*SNF* 374).[9]

"Forms of a Legend" focuses on the story's cultural transformations. "Reality may be too complex for oral transmission; legends recreate it in a way that is only accidentally false and which permits it to travel through the world from mouth to mouth", Borges stresses in his introduction (373). He goes on to trace the story's transcultural circulation: a seventh-century Christian version, the novel of *Barlaam and Josaphat* (374), filtered into Christendom through an earlier Islamic retelling, the legend of Bilawar and Budasaf.[10] This Christian legend, in which prince Josaphat is converted by the hermit Barlaam, was itself subsequently translated into many languages including Icelandic, where it generated the thirteenth-century *Barlaam's Saga*. The hero, his Indian origin forgotten, was eventually canonized by the Vatican as Saint Josaphat. "In 1615... Diego de Couto denounced the similarity of the spurious Indian fable to the true and pious history of St. Josaphat" (375).[11] Two details are perhaps worth noting for their strong autobiographical resonance: firstly, in the Christian version, Josaphat encounters a blind man rather than an old man; secondly, the essay "Forms of a Legend" ends on a surprising note with a reference to Oscar Wilde: "At the end of the 19th century Oscar Wilde proposed a variation: The

---

[9] The essay was initially published in *La Nación*, 8 June 1952, then included in *Otras inquisiciones*, and later selected by Borges for the *Personal Anthology* in 1961: *SNF* 543 Note.

[10] The Christian version, "Saints Barlaam and Josaphat", can be found in *The Golden Legend* (Voragine 741–752). For a comprehensive study of the appropriation of the Buddha legend into Islam and Christianity, see Lopez and McCracken.

[11] Corroborating Borges's larger point about the story's circulation throughout world literature, the legend also entered the Islamic sphere in the form of the eighth century Sufi saint Ibrahim Ibn Adham: Younes 87–99.

happy prince dies in the seclusion of the palace, without having discovered sorrow, but his posthumous effigy discerns it from atop his pedestal" (376). It is well known that Borges's first publication, at the age of nine, was a translation of Oscar Wilde's children's story "The Happy Prince".[12]

Published a year later, "The Dialogues of Ascetic and King"[13] focuses on the archetypal significance of the king's fourth and final encounter, with the ascetic. "A king is a plenitude, an ascetic is nothing or wants to be nothing, and so people enjoy imagining a dialogue between these two archetypes. Here are a few examples, from Eastern and Western sources". Among these Borges lists Diogenes Laërtius's *Lives of the Philosophers*, the first-century Buddhist text *Milinda Pañha*, and various Chinese or Scandinavian incarnations. The Buddha himself, fittingly, remains unnamed, and is only alluded to as "another king of the Sanscrit era who left his palace to beg alms in the streets, and who said these dizzying words: 'From now on I have no kingdom, or my kingdom is limitless; from now on my body does not belong to me or the whole earth belongs to me'" (384).[14]

Once again Borges's attention is on the motif's transcultural circulation. The essay's conclusion invokes a Goethean model of literary circulation: "These texts, scattered in time and space, suggest the possibility of a morphology (to use Goethe's word) or science of the fundamental forms of literature. I have occasionally speculated in these pages that all metaphors are variants of a small number of archetypes; perhaps this proposition is also applicable to fables" (385).

Goethe's morphology, originally developed in the context of his botanical studies published in *The Metamorphosis of Plants*, proposed to account for "the laws of metamorphosis by which nature produces one part through another, creating a great variety of forms through the modification of a single organ".[15] Extending the comparative anatomical model, Goethe proposed the idea of an archetype from which an infinite variety of plant and animal forms could potentially

---

[12] "El príncipe feliz", *El País*, Buenos Aires, 25 June 1910. The translation was mistakenly attributed to his father, Jorge Guillermo Borges: Borges (1970: 211). Wilde's story is discussed in Chapter 2.

[13] "The Dialogues of Ascetic and King", *SNF* 383.

[14] This is repeated in the late parable "The Mirror and the Mask": see Chapter 3.

[15] Goethe (1995: 76).

derive.[16] The appropriation of the morphological model from the natural world (botany, anatomy) to the world of art (history, literature), which was never explicitly or systematically mapped out by Goethe,[17] was nevertheless attempted by several later thinkers who, in some cases, took the analogy further than Goethe himself. Interest in Goethe's scientific works was renewed in the 1920s by a series of critical editions, and the morphological model variously applied to history (Oswald Spengler) and literary criticism (Günther Müller, André Jolles, or, on the opposite side of the political spectrum, Vladimir Propp).[18] Borges was familiar with the work of Spengler, for whom Goethe was a key influence, and who subtitled his 1918 *Decline of the West "Outlines of a Morphological World History"* in explicit reference to Goethe. One of Borges's capsule biographies, published in 1936, is devoted to Spengler, mentioning in particular his ambition to "lay down the foundations of a morphology of cultures".[19] Spengler's attempt to seek the type beyond the accident could appeal to Borges

[16] Goethe revealed his discovery of the *Urpflanze* in a letter to Johann Gottfried Herder in 1787, during his Italian journey which was the major catalyst for his scientific intuition: "With this model and the key to it an infinite number of additional plants can be invented". He later postulated an analogous animal archetype in his 1795 "Outline for a General Introduction to a Comparative Anatomy" (Goethe 1995: xx).

[17] In his Preface to *On Morphology*, Goethe acknowledged moving analogically from botany to anatomy: "In the process I was soon obliged to postulate a prototype against which all mammals could be compared as to points of agreement or divergence. As I had earlier sought out the archetypal plant I now aspired to find the archetypal animal; in essence, the concept or idea of the animal" (Goethe 1995: 69). In his conversations with Herder, who was at the time writing his *Ideas on the Philosophy of the History of Mankind*, Goethe also envisioned applying the morphological model to human history. A fragment of *Studies for a Physiology of Plants* sketches out a parallel between nature and art: "Example of a city as the work of man. Example of the metamorphosis of insects as the work of nature" (Goethe 1995: 75).

[18] On the revival of Goethean morphology in Germany in the 1920s, and its subsequent appropriation (and distortion) by various historians and literary critics, see Neubauer (1988: 263) and especially (1998: 223–226).

[19] "Oswald Spengler", *SNF* 170. Spengler's morphological view of history is also alluded to in "Theme of the Traitor and the Hero": investigating Fergus Kilpatrick's death, his biographer Ryan, struck by the parallels with Caesar's story, is reminded of "the morphologies proposed by Hegel, Spengler and Vico" (*CF* 144). A later essay on Nathaniel Hawthorne further corroborates this view, remembering Schopenhauer's kaleidoscope metaphor for history, where infinite configurations of events result from a finite number of glass pieces (*OC* 2: 57), see Introduction.

as germane to his own plot-centered model of narrative. It is conceivable that Borges was also aware of German critics' attempts to found a morphological literary theory, such as Günther Müller's "morphological poetics" or André Jolles's 1930 *Einfache Formen* [Simple Forms],[20] although obviously Borges would not have shared their political beliefs. Perhaps indeed Borges's allusion to morphology was a way of pushing back against the political misuse of Goethe's ideas.[21]

In addition—confirming that Goethe's morphology is not intrinsically linked to right-wing ideology—Borges's modular view of literary composition also brings to mind Vladimir Propp's work on folktales: whether or not Borges had actually read Propp, they share the Goethean reference, of foundational importance for Propp. Goethe's famous statement, "the study of forms is the study of transformations",[22] served as an epigraph to Propp's book, which also abounds in quotations from Goethe on problems of morphology and metamorphosis.[23] Borges's hypothesis on "fables" (narratives or plots) as "variants of a small number of archetypes", although lightly touched on and left undeveloped, with characteristic reticence, closely resembles Propp's metaphor of the "compositional scheme" as the plot's "skeleton": "the common compositional scheme that lies at the basis of fairy tales... does not exist in reality. But it is realized in the narrative in the most diverse forms; it lies at the basis of plots; it is, so to speak, their skeleton".[24] Borges formulated his basic ideas—archetypal stories; writing as rewriting—very

---

[20] A discussion of Jolles's "simple forms" can be found in Scholes 42–50. A revised edition of Jolles's book appeared in 1956, contemporary with Borges's essays.

[21] Wellek and Warren's *Theory of Literature*, which cautioned against transdisciplinary distortions of biological models, is also contemporary with Borges's essays (see Neubauer 1998: 228, Note 19).

[22] In a 1796 handwritten note to the *Morphology*. quoted in Engelstein 28.

[23] The importance of the Goethe-Propp connection is discussed by yet another writer whose work Borges was certainly aware of, although he did not mention him in his essays: anthropologist Mircea Eliade. Writing in 1951 after a visit to the Palermo botanical garden, and recalling Goethe's earlier and famous botanical epiphany in an Italian garden, Eliade acknowledges both the significance of Goethe's morphology for Propp's critical work and its relevance as a hermeneutic model not only for the natural world, but for spiritual creations as well, in particular for his own field: Spineto 370–372. On the correspondences between Borges's archetypal theory of narrative and Eliade's *Myth of the Eternal Return*, see Christ 33–34 and 217.

[24] Quoted in Toporov 255.

early in his career, arriving, perhaps independently, at some of the same conclusions as Propp (and, we might add, the Russian Formalists, whose theories, particularly Shklovsky's conception of poetry as disposition and re-elaboration of images, expressed in his 1917 essay "Art as Technique", also seem germane).[25]

Although we lack evidence that Borges had firsthand knowledge of Goethe's scientific work, in particular *Morphology of Plants* where the idea of archetypal unity and dynamic transformation of plant forms is developed, we may surmise that Borges knew enough—directly or indirectly—to draw an analogy between Goethe's morphology and his own morphological views of literature. In an essay on metaphor written in 1952 (the Buddha years), but later collected with earlier essays on poetry in *History of Eternity*, Borges sketched out the idea of universal poetry as the circulation of fundamental metaphors morphing into one another. Enumerating variations on the death-as-sleep metaphor and the woman-as-flower metaphor from the Bible and the *Iliad* on, Borges concludes that, from a very small number of archetypal images, "unlimited" poetic possibilities can derive.[26]

It appears, then, that when Borges mentions Goethe's morphology in the context of an essay on Buddhism, his reflections on Buddhism are intertwined with his view of literature as infinite variations on a finite—indeed minuscule—number of basic modules, whether metaphors or plots. Literature in general is essentially a repetition: "perhaps universal

---

[25] "The images a given poet used and which you thought his own were taken almost unchanged from another poet... poets are much more concerned with arranging images than with creating them" (Shklovsky 7). Sturrock (212–213) stresses the role of Eikhenbaum's serial narrative principle. Despite similar conceptions of poetry as re-elaboration and disposition of images, Alazraki (1990: 104) argues against a direct influence of the Russian Formalists on Borges, because their writings would be translated only after the war, when Victor Erlich and Roman Jakobson introduced them to American scholars. What is certain, however, is that later literary critics, in particular Tzvetan Todorov and Gérard Genette, would bring together the ideas of the Russian Formalists and those of Borges, ensuring a key place for Borges in the history of Structuralism and Post-Structuralism. On hypertextuality as "open Structuralism" and Borges's place in this configuration, see Genette (1997: ix and 251–254).

[26] "Ello no significa, naturalmente, que se haya agotado el número de metáforas; los modos de indicar, o insinuar estas secretas simpatías de los conceptos resultan, de hecho, ilimitados" ("La metáfora", *Historia de la eternidad*, OC 2: 384). One of the Charles Eliot Norton lectures that Borges delivered at Harvard in 1967–1968, "The Metaphor", expanded and illustrated the same idea: Borges (2000: 21–41).

history is the history of the diverse intonation of a few metaphors", he concludes at the end of the 1951 essay "Pascal's Sphere" (*SNF* 353). The fictions repeatedly bear out this idea of all possible stories as "virtually inexhaustible repetitions, versions, perversions" of the same few archetypes.[27] A later prose poem, "Los cuatro ciclos", from *El oro de los tigres* (1972), revisits the paradigm of the four archetypal stories (a doomed city; a return journey; a quest; a sacrificed god) from which all others derive: "Four are the stories", the poem concludes. "During the time that we have left we will go on telling them, transformed."[28] The same holds true of poetry, defined in strong opposition to originality in "Ars poetica": "To see in death sleep, and in the sunset / A sad gold—such is poetry, / Which is immortal and poor. Poetry / Returns like the dawn and the sunset" (*SP* 137). This even holds true of Borges's essays, in which philosophical theories, ideas, and images, from disparate origins and traditions, fluidly and incessantly morph into one another.[29] The writer's task is not to invent new metaphors, new stories, new ideas, but to rewrite old ones.[30]

1.3   *Borgesian* Weltliteratur

Whether influence or coincidence, then, these various "morphological" views of literature as repetition and rewriting intersect. More importantly, they all hark back to Goethe's organic conception of *Weltliteratur*.[31] Perhaps it is also typical of Borges that a key piece of the

---

[27] "A Biography of Tadeo Isidoro Cruz (1829–1874)", *CF* 212.

[28] Translation mine. In the original: "Cuatro son las historias. Durante el tiempo que nos queda seguiremos narrándolas, transformadas" (*OC* 2: 506). The same idea is emphasized in Borges's interview with Jacques Chancel: "I do not write, I rewrite... We are all the heirs of millions of scribes who have already written down all that is essential a long time before us. We are all copyists, and all the stories have already been told. There are no longer any original ideas" (Chancel 1999: 74; quoted in Kristal 2002: 135).

[29] Borges's theories are "never fixed, never final, always fluid and always susceptible to further alterations": Flynn 23.

[30] On this key aspect of Borges's aesthetic, see in particular Lafon, Alazraki (1990) and Regazzoni (1999: 555–564). More recently, cognitive approaches to narratology seem to offer new and productive ways of revisiting Borges's archetypal theories, see Conclusion, p. 135.

[31] The similarity with Auerbach's manifesto "Philology and *Weltliteratur*", published a year later (1952) is also striking: "Our philological home is the earth: it can no longer be the nation" (Auerbach 73).

intellectual puzzle (the hypothesis of a Goethean "morphology... or science of the fundamental forms of literature") is tossed in almost as an afterthought and left undeveloped in the essay's concluding sentence. Yet Borges's affinities with the inventor of *Weltliteratur* cannot be overestimated. Borges intuited world literature as a network of circulating forms—although obviously with a much broader, less Eurocentric reach, reflecting the hundred years of ever-increasing globalization elapsed since Goethe first envisioned *Weltliteratur*.[32] The historical situation of Borges in post-war Argentina parallels Goethe's in post-Napoleonic Germany in important ways. Both writers resisted narrow-minded nationalism and sought to reach beyond linguistic borders. Their familiarity with several languages and literary traditions was also a political statement. According to Fritz Strich, Goethe thought it "the duty of every true friend of the Fatherland to discard the petty restrictions of linguistic patriotism and to foster the spread of foreign languages... in contrast to the exaggerated nationalism of post-Napoleonic Germany".[33] Goethe's subsequent opposition to German Romantic nationalism also echoes Borges's anti-nationalist polemics in "The Argentine Writer and Tradition".[34]

In addition, both writers assigned a vital role to translations and the press in the process of literary circulation. Goethe's lifelong work as a polyglot translator was enhanced by a wealth of theoretical reflections on the art of translating, disseminated throughout his writings.[35] For Goethe, the translator is "a mediator in this universal, intellectual trade", who "makes it his business to promote exchange"; despite their shortcomings, translations "are and will remain most important and worthy undertakings in world communication".[36] Goethe was well aware that translations could

---

[32] George Steiner, however, stresses the breadth and reach of Goethe's *Weltliteratur*, noting that Goethe translated for over 73 years, from 18 languages, and although in some cases the translations were secondary, "nevertheless, the range of linguistic-literary awareness and active involvement is formidable" (Steiner 261). For a more recent reappraisal of *Weltliteratur's* global reach, see Pizer 25–28.

[33] Strich 33–34. Strich's book, which Borges may very well have read, was published directly after the war, and has strong symbolic resonances with Goethe's own historical situation. Honoring the founder of *Weltliteratur* after the defeat of Nazi Germany made a compelling universalist statement in favor of cultural tolerance and diversity: Steiner 268.

[34] Aizenberg (48–50), Woodall (185–186) and Sarlo (26–28) all contextualize that essay within the contemporary debate between Borges and nationalist critics.

[35] Berman 88.

[36] Goethe (1986: 207).

reinvigorate originals, including his own works: "Goethe's idea, as new as it was stimulating, was that translations confer benefits in both directions".[37] The influential definition of world literature as literature that gains in translation, proposed by David Damrosch at the beginning of the millennium, has roots in both Goethe and Borges.[38] Conversely, Goethe's eleven points on *Weltliteratur* sketch the prehistory of today's global information age: in a world of "ever-increasing ease of communication", where "any work is readily obtainable", a writer has a duty to be informed and to inform about the foreign press and the international book trade.[39]

Borges too, well into the fifties (until blindness interfered) was just such an intellectual mediator. We need only to think of Borges's enormous output as a reviewer of foreign books and films, and of course his important *œuvre* as a translator of Kafka, Woolf, Faulkner, Michaux, Poe, and Snorri Sturluson, among others.[40] However, while both writers championed an ecumenical view of world literature as dialogue, exchange, intercourse between nations, Borges did not share Goethe's idealistic humanism. For Goethe, world literature was the happy outcome of wars, which force nations into cultural contact: "All nations, thrown together at random by terrible wars, then reverting to their status as individual nations, could not help realizing that they had been subjected to foreign influences, had absorbed them and occasionally become aware of intellectual needs previously unknown. The result was a sense of goodwill. Instead of isolating themselves as before, their state of mind has gradually developed a desire to be included in the free exchange of ideas".[41]

For Goethe, the political benefit of world literature equaled, perhaps surpassed, its cultural value.[42] Borges, in contrast, did not believe that

---

[37] Strich 21. Berman (104–109) stresses Goethe's innovative and fundamental conception of translation as regeneration. Borges too praised translations of his own works enthusiastically.

[38] Although Damrosch's focus is on Goethe's *Weltliteratur*, while Borges is only mentioned briefly on two occasions (Damrosch 2003: 97, 262).

[39] Goethe (1986: 227 and 226) respectively. On Goethe's involvement with the cultural networks of his time, translations and the press, see Damrosch 1–14 and Guillén 145–146.

[40] Kristal (2002: 39–41).

[41] Goethe (1986: 228).

[42] According to John Gearey, the ultimate purpose of Goethe's *Weltliteratur* is social and political ("Postscript", Goethe 1986: 240). Pizer also points to the desire for peace as "a core motivating factor" for Goethe's *Weltliteratur* (21).

world literature could bolster world peace.[43] With the dubious privilege of hindsight that came from living and writing in a century of two world wars, Borges took a more apolitical view of world literature, one both more and less radical than Goethe's. On the one hand, it is more inclusive than Goethe's: in particular, it offers a rewarding postcolonial model, since the innovative edge in world literature is ascribed, not to cultures that enjoy a central position like Germany for Goethe, but on the contrary, to groups that enjoy the paradoxical benefits of marginality, such as the Irish, Jews, or South Americans, whose "irreverence" and lack of "superstition" with respect to the dominant tradition allows them the greater freedom of recreating it from the margins (*SNF* 426).[44] Borges's argument anticipates the one Deleuze and Guattari would later develop in their influential essay on "minor literature", taking Kafka as their case study.[45]

On the other hand, Borges's view of world literature reveals a shifting and paradoxical relationship to historical particulars. At times, he problematizes the connection between a text and its specific historical period—as in "Pierre Menard, Author of the *Quixote*", which takes to its limits the idea that a text's meaning is dependent on historical context. At other times, his model of world literature is one in which the repetition of narrative and/or poetic forms ("metaphors" and "fables") erodes and renders inessential the specific historical, political or cultural contexts. This timeless conception of world literature *sub specie aeternitatis* is the one that prevails in the speculations on the Renunciation legend. This, then, is the paradox of Borges's *Weltliteratur*—a utopian view of world literature, unmoored from space and time, distilled into a pure essence, from which the 'world', both in the geographical and the metaphysical sense, has been abstracted.[46]

---

[43] Borges shares this skeptical view with Auerbach, for whom contemporary *Weltliteratur* is "less practical, less political", and no longer aims at "spiritual exchange between peoples" or "the reconciliation of races" (Auerbach 2012: 68).

[44] On Borges's interest in Judaism as a paradigm for Argentine postcolonial cultural identity, see Aizenberg's seminal analysis, especially vii–viii and 3–53.

[45] Deleuze and Guattari (1975). On the concept of minor literature applied to Borges, see De Toro 68–110, Waisman 132 and Jullien (2007: 205–223).

[46] On Borges's "absolute antihistoricism" in connection to Buddhism, see Paoli 184. This, of course, is an important difference between Borges's and Goethe's conceptions of world literature, since Goethe understood *Weltliteratur* as an essentially contemporary phenomenon linked to the emergence of a world market for the trade of spiritual as well as material goods: Berman 90–91. More on Borges's a-historicism in Chapter 2.

1.4   A Morphological Conception of Literary Inventio

Borges's morphological speculation—that "metaphors" and "fables" are "variants of a small number of archetypes" (*SNF* 385)—commands two important consequences: it provides both a reading ethos for Borges the reader (reading for the plot in narratives, extracting the core metaphor in poetry and the recurrent idea in essays), and a writing praxis for Borges the writer (*inventio* conceived as variations on archetypes). The parable titled "The Plot" (from *The Maker*) turns explicitly on the idea that stories are generated by repeating archetypal plots with circumstantial variations. Attacked by his godson, the gaucho dies "so that a scene [Julius Caesar's murder at the hands of Brutus] can be played out again" (*CF* 307). Here as often, the transformation is obtained by transcultural variation—transposing the archetypal plot from ancient Rome to nineteenth-century Argentina—a strategy that illustrates and furthers the anti-nationalist agenda of "The Argentine Writer and Tradition". An earlier story, "Theme of the Traitor and the Hero" fictionalizes the idea of "a secret shape of time, a pattern of repeating lines". Once again Caesar's archetypal death is repeated in a different space-time as the Irish rebel Fergus Kilpatrick's death, and the narrator acknowledges "the morphologies proposed by Hegel, Spengler, and Vico" as well as "the transmigration of souls" (*CF* 144). Both history and story follow the morphological rule of archetype-and-variation. Reading for both entails a process of abstraction, from multiplicity to unity; writing, conversely, a process of expansion, from unity to multiplicity.

Renunciation stories follow the same pattern. The archetype—the king leaving his palace after encountering an ascetic, to become a wandering beggar—branches off into a multiplicity of variants. Three parables, spanning over thirty years of Borges's writing, "The Two Kings and the Two Labyrinths", "Parable of the Palace", and "The Mirror and the Mask", display exemplary chronological spread and transcultural breadth. Reading morphologically enables extraction of the common archetype: an (initially Indian) story of kingly dispossession is recast as Arabian, Chinese and Irish stories, all accidental variations on the plot. The kingly figure who has everything—the Babylonian king, the Yellow Emperor, the Irish king—loses to the ascetic figure who has little or nothing: the Arabian king, the Chinese poet, the Irish poet. Each time, the king's confidence is shattered by the ascetic figure, who reveals to him the "nothingness"[47] of his kingdom. In "The Two Kings and the Two Labyrinths", the Arab king proves to the Babylonian king that a vast expanse of empty sand can be even more labyrinthine than the elaborate edifice built by his architects. In "Parable of the Palace", the Yellow Emperor loses his palace when the Poet recites an Aleph-like poem which, despite its brevity (a single line or word) contains "the entire enormous palace, whole and to the last detail" (318). In "The Mirror and the Mask", after the final confrontation with the poet, the king leaves his palace to become "a beggar who wanders the roads of Ireland, which once was his kingdom" (454).[48]

That reading and writing develop along morphological lines is made clear in the table of contents of Borges's *Personal Anthology*. The stories are not arranged chronologically—showing Borges's indifference to the individual writer's development in favor of the stories' generative process—but rather according to an order of "sympathies and differences" (*PA* ix), which showcases common meaning: "Sometimes I find out that I've written the same parable or story twice over or that two different stories carry the same meaning, and so I try to put them alongside each other (...) After all, I think that a poet has maybe five or six poems to write and not more than that. He's trying his hand at writing them from different angles and perhaps with different plots and in different ages and different characters, but the poems are essentially and innerly the same".[49] Beyond a simple thematic similarity—"Biography of Tadeo Isidoro Cruz" (*PA* 161) and "The End" (*PA* 166) are both continuations of the *Martín Fierro* epic; "Story of the Warrior and the Captive" (*PA* 170) and "The Captive" (*PA* 175) both deal with the civilization vs. barbarity dialectic, the master trope of Argentine historiography; "*Inferno* I, 32" (*PA* 80) and "The Other Tiger" (*PA* 81) are both tiger stories, etc.—they all repeat the fundamental pattern of *coincidentia oppositorum*, the hero's conversion into his opposite: from soldier to

---

[47] In an early essay, "La nadería de la personalidad" (first published in *Proa* in 1922 and later included in *Inquisiciones*, translated as "The Nothingness of Personality" and included in *SNF* 3), Borges used the word to substantiate an absence, as if to suggest an equivalence between "everything" and "nothing"—not coincidentally, the title of another famous text ("Everything and Nothing"), which immediately follows "Parábola del palacio" in *El Hacedor* (*OC* 2: 181).

[48] I revisit these stories later, in Chapters 3 and 4.

[49] Christ 283.

rebel ("Tadeo Isidoro Cruz"), from murderer to victim ("The End"), from white to Indian, from Barbarian to city-dweller, from traitor to hero, from king to beggar, and so forth. The conversion can take place within the same story (in "The Warrior and the Captive", the Barbarian who dies defending Ravenna faces the English woman who chooses the Indians), or from one story to the next. "The Captive", the story of a white boy lost to the wild, repeats the previous plot with circumstantial differences. "*Inferno* I, 32", a parable about a real animal turned into a poem, sits next to a poem about a real animal who eludes poetic efforts to capture it in verse.[50] Contiguity ("I try to put them alongside each other") works to underscore archetypal continuity beneath accidental variations.

2   "ETHICS FOR IMMORTALS": BUDDHISM, IMPERSONALITY, AND THE NOVEL

The impersonality of literature, and the rejection of the psychological novel, are foundational Borgesian ideas: central, recurrent, and linked. "Dialogues of Ascetic and King" is about archetypes: the Ascetic and the King are not psychological characters but allegorical entities, agents, roles such as Borges uses in his own fictions, where psychology plays no part, and the emphasis is entirely on plot. An earlier essay, "Personality and the Buddha",[51] after summarizing the main facts of the Renunciation story, spells out the Buddhist ideal of impersonality and connects it explicitly with the rejection of the Western novelistic tradition, which is based on the antithetical axiom of individual singularity: "The path of purity reads: 'In no place am I something for someone, nor is anyone something for me; to believe that one's self is an I—*attavada*—is the worst heresy for Buddhism'" (*SNF* 349). Borges concludes: "From Chaucer to Marcel Proust, the novel's substance is the unrepeatable, the singular flavor of souls; for Buddhism there is no such flavor, or it is one of the many vanities of the cosmic simulacrum" (350).

---

[50] In addition to chronological indifference, the table of contents also juxtaposes stories, essays and poems without regard for generic taxonomies: parables about authorial dispossession ("The Maker", "Everything and Nothing") are positioned next to the essay on Shakespeare "From Someone to No One", for instance.

[51] First published in *Sur*, nos. 192–194, 1950, but not reprinted since nor included in the *Obras completas*: see the Note, *SNF* 542.

The ideal of impersonality recurs with repetitions and variations across essays, lectures and interviews.[52] In a kind of Borgesian version of the Platonic trinity, philosophical, ethical, and aesthetic principles converge.[53] In "Personality and the Buddha", Borges refers to Catholic writer Léon Bloy (often mentioned in the essays for his outrageously polemical views and as a paradoxical continuator of the Cabalists).[54] Casting Buddha "as a critic of Western literature",[55] Borges condemns Bloy's baroque style, "in which each sentence seeks to shock us", as "morally inferior" for "elaborating, within the common language, a small and vain dialect" (*SNF* 350), in violation of the Buddhist ideal of self-dispossession, which straddles ethics and aesthetics. Another writer, much more famous than Léon Bloy, comes to mind: James Joyce, with whom Borges had a tormented relationship—admiring his poetic genius and his early stories, for example, but also ultimately condemning him for the same fault, repeatedly dismissing *Ulysses* and *Finnegans Wake* as unreadable.[56] Naturally, Borges the minimalist was bothered by the sheer length of Joyce's novels (or for that matter, Proust's). More importantly, we may surmise that Borges's strong disavowal of Joyce's stylistic excess originated in an uneasy mix of identification (with the polyglot, the de-centered Irishman, the blind writer) and rejection. Borges thought himself guilty of the same sin—the "small and vain dialect", the baroque style he favored in his youth and of which he rigorously and painstakingly stripped himself, going to great lengths to dissociate himself from and eliminate any traces of the young, flamboyant Borges.[57] In the Prologue to *The Self and the Other*, Borges reiterated this idea in terms

---

[52] The late lecture on Buddhism (*SN* 58–75) covers many of the same points but also goes deeper into questions of doctrine. Both this lecture and the conversation with C. Parodi and I. Almeida (2005: 101–124) commend Buddhism as a religion that does not require an act of faith in its story or its character, since the historical individuality of Buddha is irrelevant, even illusory.

[53] On the interface of Buddhism with literary creation, see San Francisco, especially 148–151.

[54] See in particular "El espejo de los enigmas", *OC* 2: 98–100.

[55] Balderston (1987: 77).

[56] A highly critical review of *Finnegans Wake* appeared in 1939: "El último libro de Joyce" (*OC* 4: 535). Vincent Message (3–18) interprets "The Two Kings and the Two Labyrinths", which was written directly after this negative review, as a metaphor for the contrast between the laborious Joycean labyrinth and the minimalist Borgesian labyrinth.

[57] Williamson (2004: ix).

of a writer's destiny: "The fate of a writer is strange. He begins his career by being a baroque writer, pompously baroque, and after many years, he might attain if the stars are favorable, not simplicity, which is nothing, but rather a modest and secret complexity".[58] The self-dispossession at the heart of the Buddhist journey was also, for Borges, an exercise in eradication of authorial self-centeredness, a form of literary renunciation. Later in his life he would discover Zen Buddhism—both *QB* and "Buddhism" (*SN* 58–75) devote the final section to Zen and the post-rational process of *satori*—and try his hand at the pared-down intensity of *haiku*—*La cifra* (1981) contains 17 *haiku*—thus intensifying the asceticism and minimalism of his aesthetic ideal.[59]

If it is "morally inferior" for a writer to depart stylistically from the common language, conversely, "The Immortal", the opening story in *The Aleph* (1949), is described in the Afterword as an attempt to outline "an ethics of immortality" (*CF* 287). In this allegorical story, the identities of all writers merge into one impersonal Immortal who is Homer and No One.[60] The same moral dimension is central to "The Maker"—a reworking of "The Immortal" in parable form—in which the accidents of life (the onset of blindness, but also the individual events seared into Homer's memory) must be transcended in order to achieve the impersonal essence of literary creation.[61]

3   RENUNCIATION, POLITICS, BLINDNESS

The figure of Buddha as Renouncer and the motif of withdrawal from politics also takes on a new urgency and a heightened significance in the context of Argentina's chaotic political history. Although Borges maintained a lifelong interest in Buddhism, it intensified during periods of crushing political disappointment: in the early fifties after Perón's grip on Argentina tightened, then again some twenty years later when a military Junta imposed right-wing terror on Argentina, leading Borges to the

---

[58] *SP* 149.

[59] On *haiku*, see Kodama (1986: 170–181).

[60] On "The Immortal" as an allegory of literary creation, see Christ 207–246 and Jullien (1995: 136–159).

[61] Similarly, "Averroes' Search", also from *The Aleph*, claims impersonality and universality on behalf of poetry: "The image that only a single man can shape is the image that interests no man" (*CF* 240).

humiliating and devastating realization that the generals, whose arrival he had initially welcomed, were "gangsters" with none of the ancestral heroic virtues he had celebrated in his poetry.[62] It is perhaps no coincidence that his longest text on Buddhism, *QB*, as well as the lecture collected in *SN*,[63] belong to the darkest decade of Argentina's history: a time when Borges, now internationally famous but also blind and out of touch with his own society, was slowly and painfully amputating himself from dreams of military glory that had been his since childhood, and despairing of a peaceful political solution to the nation's woes.[64] The essays on Buddhism probe the wrenching issues of art and power; Buddhism's negation of individual attachment, whether to self or nation, seems to offer perhaps the only possible consolation, in the form of apolitical withdrawal.

The Fifties (the Buddha years) were a major turning point in Borges's life and work. Politically, Borges, along with some of his friends and relatives, suffered under Perón's dictatorship[65]; personally, the precipitous decline of his eyesight dealt a devastating blow to his life as a writer. With the onset of near-total blindness, renunciation tropes took on a more acute personal meaning. In 1955 Borges was made director of the National Library and went blind[66]: these two contradictory events (gift of the books, withdrawal of eyesight) are explicitly and symbolically linked in Borges's retelling of them. In those years he published the essays on Buddhism—which all recount the Renunciation story—alongside essays on the impersonality of literature, followed by the parable "The Maker", a meditation on Homer's legendary blindness. Taken together, these different texts corroborate the often quoted Borgesian statement that

---

[62] Slavuski 11, quoted in Williamson (2004: 459).

[63] Given as a lecture in Buenos Aires's Teatro Coliseo on 6 July 1977: *OCP* 2: 1384–1385.

[64] On this excruciating process, see Williamson's remarkable analysis, "Deconstructing the Nation" (Williamson 2004: 452–467), which gives a more nuanced view of Borges's political evolution than Alazraki (1988: 187).

[65] Williamson (2004: 322) interprets "Dialogues of Ascetic and King" in terms of Borges's opposition to Perón. Also see Williamson (2007: 288–294) for an intersecting reading of the essay and the story "The End" in the context of Borges's opposition to Perón.

[66] Like his father before him, Borges had always had poor eyesight, and it had been steadily deteriorating in the early fifties. On the 1954 accident that precipitated a state of near-total blindness, see Williamson (2004: 324).

"all literature is autobiographical".[67] They rework the Buddhist Renunciation narrative, yet they also complicate it because they are masked self-portraits and allegories of writing. In "Poem of the Gifts", which recapitulates in poetic form the creative triad of destiny, impersonality, and blindness, Borges reflects on the irony which granted him "books and blindness in one touch". Like Buddha, he will go from having everything to having nothing: "Cultures of East and West, the entire atlas, / encyclopedias, centuries, dynasties, / symbols, the cosmos, and cosmogonies / are offered from the walls, all to no purpose".[68] Crowned king of this infinite kingdom—"the universe, which others call the Library", as another famous story begins[69]—only to wander blindly along its "hollow twilight", dispossessed and beggared, the poet merges with another blind librarian, his predecessor Paul Groussac, as their identities are fused by eternity: "Which of the two is setting down this poem— / a single sightless self, a plural I? / What can it matter, then, the name that names me, / given our curse is common and the same?" (SP 97).

Buddhism, a lifelong engagement, became ever more central to Borges's preoccupations in those later years. It offered both a model for world literature and an abstract image of destiny, and tied his view of literature as transmigration and circulation of "fables" and "metaphors" across time and space—ever more distant from author or context as it grew into an expansive network of anonymous texts—to an intensified spiritual quest.[70] An accident of life led him to privilege certain idiosyncratic features, in particular brevity, orality, and repetition, in his own creative process. By reverting to a form of semi-oral

---

[67] Quoted in Williamson (2004: ix, xxii, etc.). Naturally, autobiography here is not to be taken in any confessional sense, but rather as an ironic construct about the paradoxes of authorship, as a parable such as "Borges and I" (CF 124) demonstrates.

[68] SP 95.

[69] "The Library of Babel", CF 112.

[70] Suzanne Jill Levine refers to Borges's "multiple and contradictory personae: the agnostic priest of literature, the ascetic homo ludens, the blind seer, the intellectual mystic, and perhaps ultimately, the soul-seeking skeptic" (Borges et al. 2010: xix). A recent trend of criticism focuses on Borges's spirituality and mysticism: see in particular Flynn (2009), who privileges the Christian perspective in Borges's final years, and Bossart (2003), who, in a final section, highlights the Buddhist dimension of Borges's spiritual trajectory.

composition (dictations, lectures and interviews), governed by the modes of variation, repetition and improvisation, Borges returned, circuitously, to the fundamentals of literature. Scheherazade, the ancient bards, the nameless *confabulatores nocturni* of the parable titled "Alguien" from *History of the Night*,[71] became Borges's preferred models—unseating the earlier, written encyclopedic model, and leaving far behind the sovereign paradigms of nationality and authorship.

---

[71] "Alguien" imagines the origin of the *1001 Nights: OC* 3: 171.

CHAPTER 2

A Lesson for the King: Renunciation and Politics

Abstract This chapter follows the political thread that runs through the story, interrogating its purpose as a didactic tool. Renunciation stories are told to kings in an attempt to control or mitigate their tyrannical behavior. The king-and-ascetic dialogue sets up a confrontation between power and authority, which paradoxically the king loses to a powerless adversary. This chapter explores how Renunciation stories can be used to achieve political goals, with renouncer figures serving as instruments of awareness in political genres—fables or mirrors for princes. The discussion reaches beyond Borges to a constellation of stories from the Borgesian hypertext (from Burton's hermit trilogy in the *1001 Nights* to Victorian renouncer stories) that complicate the pen-vs-sword problem. Ultimately, Renunciation stories raise the bigger questions of the power of storytelling and the possibility of truth-telling that were also central preoccupations for Hannah Arendt and Michel Foucault. It also reassesses Borges's ambiguous position against this rich political tradition.

Keywords Mirror for princes · Parrhesia · *1001 Nights* · Fables · Political · Apolitical · Burton · Wilde · Kipling · Arendt · Foucault

© The Author(s) 2019
D. Jullien, *Borges, Buddhism and World Literature*, Literatures of the Americas, https://doi.org/10.1007/978-3-030-04717-7_2

After two days of discussion, or catechism, he converted the king, who put on the yellow robe of a Buddhist monk.[1]

The previous chapter explored the links between the Buddhist Renunciation legend and Borges's morphological view of literature as infinite variations on a finite number of archetypal "fables". It also introduced the motif of political detachment. This chapter focuses on the political power of the renunciation story. On the one hand, the story sets up a basic confrontation between a figure of absolute power—a king—and a figure of absolute powerlessness—an ascetic. The powerless contestant paradoxically wins; the moral dismisses power as illusory. On the other hand, the story is often used as a teaching story for the powerful: in this way, it is close to other pedagogical genres such as the fable or the mirror for princes. Stories about ascetics, about renouncing kings, are powerful stories that have, or aim to have political outcomes, exerting their pull on the imagination beyond the poetic into the political realm. How can the ascetic's words (in Borges's essay, the "two days of discussion") convert the king? How can dialogue or storytelling exert political pressure? These Borgesian themes and more generally the king-and-ascetic dialogue intersect contemporary debates of political philosophy, in particular discussions by Hannah Arendt and Michel Foucault. The interweaving of the poetic and the political, the agency of storytelling, are also central preoccupations in Hannah Arendt's late work, surfacing in her essay on "Truth and Politics," her reflections on Karen Blixen, and elsewhere. The Greek counterpart of the ascetic speaking truth to power is the Cynic (Borges stresses the transcultural kinship repeatedly): here Borges's speculations on the pen-and-sword conundrum also anticipate much of today's resurgence of interest in Cynicism—from Foucault to Sloterdijk—as an anti-political ethos born from the ashes of ideology and the current political disillusionment.[2]

Whether the story has an otherworldly and spiritual outcome (the king's renunciation), or a worldly and political one (instructing and improving the king), hinges largely on its ending. In the otherworldly or "yellow robe" variant (Borges's Milinda story), the exit from the palace is final, as it is in the foundational Buddha legend where the king

---

[1] "The Dialogues of Ascetic and King", *SNF* 383.

[2] See "The Return of Diogenes as Postmodern Intellectual", Andreas Huyssen's Foreword to Sloterdijk ix–xxv.

forsakes political power. Siddharta leaves behind forever his life of luxury, his wife and child, his throng of concubines, his boon companions. But sometimes, after a temporary incognito outing, the king returns to his palace, made wiser by his adventures in the world of the less privileged; Harun Al-Rashid's incognito adventures in the Baghdad of the *1001 Nights* are perhaps the most famous example. This is the worldly variant, whose primarily political aim is to enlighten and teach the king, to strengthen the polis. The king's temporary renunciation is an exercise in powerlessness, whose outcome is to re-found power on a better basis.

Both variants, the abdicating king and the king in disguise, are derived from the same archetype; each tells a very different, yet equally compelling story. Both also turn on the power of story. Borges's essays on renunciation make other stories readable from the viewpoint of the power of story—from Burton's "Hermit tales" in the *Nights* to Oscar Wilde's "Happy Prince" or Kipling's *Kim*. Yet, as we will see, against the backdrop of this rich political tradition, Borges's own position (his answer, one might say, to Arendt's query) is ambiguous, both ostensibly apolitical and sharply political. He posits the confrontation repeatedly, but also appears to disengage from its circumstantial urgency. His emphasis on the story's ability to travel, adapt, hybridize, shows its resilience, its transnational relevance, its endurance through time. But it also shifts the focus away from the issue of political agency toward the poetic awareness of pattern, loosening the grip of political and historical specificity.

1   THE APPEAL OF PARADOX

"The Dialogues of Ascetic and King" captures the appeal of the infinitely adaptable renunciation story. "A king is a plenitude, an ascetic is nothing or wants to be nothing, and so people enjoy imagining a dialogue between these two archetypes" (*SNF* 382). Here is power reduced to its essence, an abstraction of the ubiquitous confrontation between rich and poor, powerful and powerless. "People enjoy" this, Borges claims, because of our natural attraction to the symbolic. Beneath the superficial differences "beats a dark opposition of symbols" (382). This pared-down version of the perennial conflict spawns the many variants listed by Borges in his essay—Greek, Indian, Chinese, or Scandinavian. What accounts for its moral appeal and political persuasiveness, I propose, is that it deploys the seduction of paradox. Contrary to expectation, it is the powerless ascetic who wins the contest. This is the turning point in the Buddha story: "On another outing, the last, he sees a monk of the mendicant orders who desires neither to live nor to die. Peace is on his face; Siddharta has found the way" (*SNF* 374). The future Buddha envies the wandering ascetic's peace of mind, the one thing he does not possess.

The first example listed in "Dialogues", the legendary encounter between Diogenes and Alexander, is borrowed from the Greek philosophical tradition. Borges's main source here is third-century Greek writer Diogenes Laertius's *Lives and Opinions of Eminent Philosophers*, which records Diogenes the Cynic's famously rude reply to Alexander the Great. In Borges's summary: "'Ask me for anything you'd like', said Alexander, and Diogenes, lying on the ground, asked him to move a little, so as not to block the light" (*SNF* 382). This celebrated legend, of which innumerable variants exist,[3] belongs to the anecdotal repertory of ancient Cynicism, with its scorn for the powerful and the political life itself. If "the zero, the ascetic, may in some way equal or surpass the infinite king" (382), it is because the strength of the (apparently weak) ascetic resides in practicing a life freed from possessions, needs and desires. Here Borges anticipates Sloterdijk's definition of philosophical wisdom as the rejection of the principle of power.[4] By spurning everything that Alexander stands for—polis, hierarchy, interdependence, customs, and conventions—Diogenes teaches the king a lesson: he is like a dog or a god, over whom the king has no power.[5]

Borges's point is not the anecdote's historical veracity—impossible to prove in any case—but rather its symbolic significance, something that also enables it to travel in time and space. In itself the encounter between Alexander and Diogenes may be a Greek reworking of a Buddhist legend[6]: thus juxtaposing Greek and Buddhist anecdotes strengthens Borges's argument both historically, as examples of Eastern influence on Western culture, and aesthetically, as evidence of the transcultural fluidity of legends.

---

[3] It is spun out by Plutarch 469, and recalled by Cicero 18: 518–519, among many others. It is also developed at length in Dio Chrysostom's fourth *Discourse*, Michel Foucault's main source for his analysis of the notion of *parrhesia* (truth telling), on which more below.

[4] "Diogenes' answer negates not only the desire for power, but the power of desire as such" (Sloterdijk 161). On the Cynic way of life, see also Kalouche 181–192.

[5] Kalouche 189. More on ancient cynicism in Chapter 3.

[6] Pizzagalli 154–160.

Borges's second example draws on the Indian tradition. In the *Milinda Pañha*, or *Questions of King Milinda*,[7] the ascetic Nagasena visited the powerful king Milinda ("Menander, the Greek king of Bactriana", whose name has been "sweetened by Oriental pronunciation" and whose fame has passed into Indian legend), and "after two days of discussion, or catechism, he converted the king, who put on the yellow robe of a Buddhist monk" (*SNF* 383). This Nagasena accomplished by showing Milinda that his kingly identity was illusory. Having no kingdom is thereby equivalent to having an infinite kingdom: King Milinda's renunciation "brings to mind another king of the Sanscrit era [Buddha, unnamed] who left his palace to beg alms in the street, and who said these dizzying words: 'From now on I have no kingdom, or my kingdom is limitless; from now on my body does not belong to me, or the whole earth belongs to me'" (384).

2   THE KING-AND-ASCETIC DIALOGUE AND THE MIRROR FOR PRINCES

The paradoxical victory of the weak over the strong, of "zero" over "infinity" (*SNF* 385) teaches the king a lesson about the limits of his power. Putting the morphological principle of pattern-and-variation into transnational practice, Borges multiplies examples of the "eternal dialogue" (383), including Heraclitus and the Persian king Darius, Boddhidharma and the Chinese emperor, and Hsiang-Lien and the Taoist beggar monk in the eighteenth-century Chinese novel *The Dream of the Red Chamber*.[8]

The pedagogical effectiveness of the king-and-ascetic model fits within a tradition of wisdom literature where stories are framed by a dialogue between a king and a wise man. For example the third-century BCE Indian classic, the *Panchatantra*, is a collection of animal fables told by

---

[7] Translated from the Pali by T. W. Rhys Davids: Müller (1879, vols. 35–36).

[8] The concluding paragraphs go further still, morphologically extending the pattern of "zero and infinity" to "a god and a dead man", which allows Borges to read the legends of Adonis, Osiris, Tammuz, and Odin as variants on the king-and-ascetic archetype. The story of Jesus is an implicit addition to this heterogeneous list. The sonnet "Juan I, 14" provides a missing link by developing an analogy between Harun al-Rashid leaving his palace in disguise to lose himself in crowd of obscure people and the incarnation of the son of god into a humble human life (*OC* 2: 271).

the legendary sage Visnu Sarma to the sons of king Amara Sakti. The pedagogical intent is explicitly stated in the Preamble: the beast fables serve both to entertain and instruct the three "supreme ignoramuses".[9] The book made its way into Persian, then Arabic, where its eighth-century reworking by Ibn Al-Muqaffa (a Persian scholar and translator living at the Abbasid court in Baghdad), known as *Kalila and Dimna*, entered European literature under the title of the *Fables of Bidpai* (or *Pilpay*), to be discovered and recreated by the likes of La Fontaine in seventeenth-century France.[10] The frame tale features an old sage, Pilpay (or Bidpai) using fables to teach king Dabschelim the art of governance.

There is of course a long and rich tradition of Western appropriation of Eastern wisdom stories, as Ros Ballaster reminds us: "European translators were not slow to see the relation between a tradition of indigenous 'Indian' writing, the *nitisastra*, a treatise on government, and the Western tradition of the *speculum principis*, or mirror for princes".[11] Animal fables were an entertaining way to instruct princes:[12] the encounter with an animal as in the inset stories, or a wise man as in the frame tale, it was hoped, would "shape a governing self" and strengthen social order.[13] In these variants, the desired outcome is not the king's conversion to an ascetic's life, but his refashioning into a better ruler thanks to storytelling. The stories themselves attempt this either by featuring a good king as a role model, or a bad one as a warning and foil.[14] The same structure is recognizable in the *1001 Nights* (a constant intertext

[9] Sarma 3.

[10] On the European translation and reception of *Kalila wa-Dimna*, see Ballaster (2005b: 43–44).

[11] Ballaster (2005b: 43).

[12] On fables as a pedagogical genre in the Arabic tradition, see Irwin (1992: 36–50).

[13] Ballaster (2005a: 358).

[14] Robert Irwin argues that *Kalila wa-Dimna* is not really a mirror for princes, since the animal kings "are usually presented in an unflattering light", contrary to the other mirrors written by Al Muqaffa, where the royal character is always a positive role model: "The animal kings tend to be capricious and stupid, and when they do act wisely it is because they have happened to take the advice of some animal wiser than themselves. For example, in *Kalila wa-Dimna* the lion king of the fable of 'The Lion and the Bull' does not act wisely or generously". Elsewhere in the work, kings are explicitly shown as greedy, capricious, or vengeful (1992: 40). I believe, however, that negative examples can be used to equal pedagogical advantage. Thus Scheherazade's stories feature both virtuous and evil women for Shahryar's edification.

and key narrative model for Borges, as is well known), where the wise Scheherazade tells stories to king Shahryar not only to entertain him, but also to improve him.

The pedagogical framework is a powerful unifying feature from the *Panchatantra* to *Kalila wa-Dimna* and the *1001 Nights*. For all its magic and extravagance, the book is also indebted to *adab* literature, the classical Arabic genre of edifying narratives intended to teach exemplary and refined behavior, both morally and culturally.[15] Scheherazade is a female version of the old ascetic,[16] with an added twist: by volunteering to marry the murderous king, she is also a variant on the renouncer hero, while her unique position as the wife of a wife-killing king makes her dramatically more vulnerable than the ascetics of either *Panchatantra* or *Kalila wa-Dimna*. Scheherazade's predicament as the disenfranchised educator of a despot is critically well established,[17] as is her frequent reliance on wisdom stories and fables. Her final success illustrates the power of story: her life has been spared, the tyrant tamed, and the tales will be recorded for the benefit of future readers.[18]

In all these stories, the didactic intent expresses itself in a frame dialogue between a powerful and a wise figure. On the one hand, these variants confirm the story's transcultural plasticity, and its powerful hold on the imagination. On the other hand, they also corroborate Hannah Arendt's insight in *The Human Condition:* stories (as opposed to novels) are associated with the political life, *vita activa* rather than *contemplativa*. In the intersubjective space of storytelling stories are shared with others, taking us out of ourselves, into the "web of human relationships" shaped by "conflicting wills and intentions".[19] Therefore storytelling represents a "strategy for

---

[15] On the origins and evolution of *adab* into a classical literary genre, and on the presence of *adab* spirit in the *1001 Nights*, see Marzolph and van Leeuwen II: 470–472, as well as Chraïbi and Sermain's introduction to Antoine Galland's translation of the *Nights*. Galland 1: iii–ix.

[16] Scheherazade is the most prominent but not the only example of wise young women in the *Nights*. On Tawadudd and other learned virgins, see Marzolph and Van Leeuwen I: 408–410.

[17] "Both stories are built on the education of rulers" and "teach through the narration of stories" (Naithani 2004: 273), see also Irwin (2004: 246–257) and Ghazoul (1996: 135).

[18] Burton's conclusion stresses the copying, storing and disseminating of the stories (X: 6).

[19] Storytelling belongs to "action", a category defined in contradistinction to "labor" (life) and "work" (production), as something that affects the polis: Arendt (1998: 184) and Wilkinson 78. Arendt was also an admirer and shrewd reader of Karen Blixen's stories: see Chapter 4.

acting on the world".[20] Some of the earliest stories in world literature show in the starkest possible form the storyteller's attempt to retain, or regain, agency, by shaping the mind and actions of an all-powerful ruler.

3   THE KING-IN-DISGUISE PARADIGM

That the ultimate goal of these stories is to improve the king is reinforced by the king-in-disguise motif. A variant on the king-and-ascetic motif is the cycle of *1001 Nights* stories involving the ninth-century caliph Harun al-Rashid, whose fame reached legendary proportions, and who enjoyed walking the streets of Baghdad incognito. In the first of the tales the caliph, who has narrowly escaped execution by the ladies' slave, summons the actors of his nocturnal adventures to the palace, and metes out rewards and punishments, bringing order, closure, and poetic justice to the stories heard the night before.[21] Stepping outside of his circle of privilege and power, impersonating a commoner within an inch of his life, made him a wiser king, ready to reassert agency and authority. Moreover, among the guests of the mysterious house are three one-eyed mendicant monks who were once kings—another reminder of the reversibility between kings and ascetics.

The caliph stories all follow the same pattern: temporary renunciation of kingly privileges followed by a return to the palace and a reassertion of authority. Despite occasional supernatural elements, these are in fact sharply political stories. Just as Siddharta discovered pain and death *extra muros*, by leaving the palace, the king discovers many things amiss in his kingdom: domestic abuse within his own inner circle,[22] corruption in his government,[23] dishonesty among the merchants,[24] even murder.[25]

---

[20] Jackson 14.

[21] The long narrative cycle is titled variously "The Story of the Three Calenders, Sons of Kings, and of the Five Ladies of Bagdad" (Galland/Mack 66–140) and "The Porter and the Three Ladies of Baghdad" Burton I: 82–186; these are the two versions discussed here, as they constitute the main references for Borges.

[22] Amine was beaten and left gruesomely scarred by her own son: "The Story of the Three Calenders", Galland/Mack 140.

[23] The Sleeper Awakened takes advantage of his day-long stint as the Caliph to punish corrupt imams: "The Story of the Sleeper Awakened", Galland/Mack 617.

[24] The Caliph gets a lesson from a working-class child on how to handle theft: "The Story of Ali Cogia, a Merchant of Bagdad", Galland/Mack 795.

[25] The discovery of a woman's corpse leads to the vizir's kitchen slave: "The Story of the Three Apples", Galland/Mack 179.

No doubt playing merchant is primarily a form of entertainment for Harun al-Rashid, who suffers from that most kingly condition, boredom and melancholy. But the game also has a serious side.[26] It is a learning experience for both kings: Harun al-Rashid, who returns to the palace a wiser king and proceeds to right wrongs, and Shahryar to whom the adventures of the good caliph are told, with the dual purpose of keeping him entertained and curing him of his murderous disposition. How does one learn to be a good king, these tales ask? By relinquishing one's kingly status, albeit temporarily; by listening to the stories of common folk outside the palace walls, like Harun al-Rashid, and to the stories told by the wise Scheherazade in the privacy of the royal bedroom—a (playful) form of spiritual–political exercise for a king.[27]

Adapted from Oriental tales, the king-in-disguise motif blossomed in European tales as well.[28] We recognize it, famously, in Shakespeare's Henry V, who goes out incognito among his soldiers the night before the fateful battle at Agincourt, at the risk of hearing candid criticism. Yet he is wise enough to reward truth-telling rather than punish it.[29] The didactic process comes full circle when he expresses a longing to be a slave instead of a king beset by anxiety.[30] So Alexander the Great wished to be Diogenes, and Siddharta a mendicant monk: the lesson learned in this transformative outing is one of renewed political self-assertion.[31]

---

[26] This is stressed by Harun al-Rashid's vizir Giafar: "Commander of the Faithful, I take the liberty to recommend to your majesty, that this is the day which you have appointed to inform yourself of the exact government of your capital city, and the little places about it, and this occasion very opportunely presents itself to dispel those clouds which could obscure your natural gaiety" ("The Adventures of Harun al-Rashid", Galland/Mack 727).

[27] Valantasis (1995: 544–552).

[28] On the political significance of the king-in-disguise motif in the context of the nineteenth-century serial novel, see Jullien (2009: 25–70).

[29] The king later forgives Williams his criticism and gives him gold (IV, 8).

[30] "Not all these, laid in bed majestical, / Can sleep so soundly as the wretched slave, / Who with a body fill'd and vacant mind / Gets him to rest..." (Henry V, IV, 1).

[31] For a reading of Shakespearean Kings and Fools in the light of Cynic parrhesia, see Hershinow 807–835.

4   BURTON'S HERMITS: REFORMING SHAHRYAR[32]

O Shahrazad, thou wouldst cause me to renounce my kingdom and thou makest me repent of having slain so many women and maidens. (Burton III: 129)

A sequence that combines beast-fables and ascetics in order to teach Shahryar a lesson is a productive case study for how tales, in particular tales about renouncers, can make kings change their ways. Burton's translation—the longest and most exhaustive, running to 16 volumes[33]—proved an inexhaustible source of narrative inspiration for Borges. It is mostly based on the 1839–1842 Calcutta II edition and contains a large number of fables.[34] These, Burton claimed in his "Terminal Essay", were an ancient literary genre quintessential to Eastern culture, born of the need to disguise political criticism, at a time when "a jealous despotism or a powerful oligarchy threw difficulties and dangers in the way of speaking 'plain truths'" (X: 115). The group of fables collected in Burton's volume III drive the political lesson home both in the stories' choice of themes and in Shahryar's dramatic reaction to them: this is the first time—after 147 nights of story-telling under threat of death—that the king expresses regret for murdering the women.[35]

The cluster of loosely interlocking stories features hermits and animals, with two nested beast-fables ("Tale of the Duck and the Peacock" and "Tale of the Birds and Beasts and the Carpenter"), followed by a series of three Hermit stories ("The Hermits"), then more beast-fables.[36] The salient features in this narrative sequence are compassion for animals and the political lesson the king appears to draw. In the central triptych, "The Hermits", proper animal husbandry is a recurring theme. The first story tells of a

---

[32] I use Burton's spelling of names in the section on Burton, and the Grub Street spelling elsewhere.

[33] Although the copy in the Borges family library was the rare 17-volume Luristan edition: Fishburn (2015: 96).

[34] The Calcutta II edition incorporated two distinct collections of fables "at some time between the 16th and the end of the 18th century": Irwin (1992: 43). On the different editions published since the nineteenth century, see Marzolph and Van Leeuwen 2: 545.

[35] In contrast to prevailing readings, Mia Gerhardt mostly dismisses attempts to analyze the king's progress toward clemency. For her, stories and frame are not interrelated (399), the stories are told in no meaningful order, and the king "rarely comments on what he has heard" (398). But this sequence of pious tales and beast fables is one such rare case when Shahryar does in fact react, strongly and meaningfully, to the stories.

[36] Encompassing Nights 145–153 in volume III: 114–162.

hermit whose pigeons thrived under his good care. The second story tells of a virtuous shepherd who tended his sheep so well that the wild beasts had no power over his flock; he was also immune to sexual temptation. In the third panel of the triptych, a pious man was told in a dream to visit the previous hermit. On the way, he rested from the heat by a fountain where birds and animals came to drink. His presence frightened them away, upon which he wept for having harmed God's creatures (III: 128). The two hermits then spent the rest of their lives together, free from society and family (III: 129).

In contrast with the rest of the *Nights*, where empathy for animals is rather rare, these stories evoke a prelapsarian world of creaturely harmony, with meek animals cared for by gentle hermits. Generically, however, fable animals traditionally represent the disenfranchised elements of society— slaves, women, subordinates in general: "fables are a form of subaltern discourse, a means of seizing verbal authority" by giving "voice to the powerless".[37] So the presence of animals in the cluster of hermit stories serves both to convey and disguise a political message. And the lesson is being heard, since for the first time, Shahryar responds to stories of cruelty toward animals by expressing regret for his cruelty toward women: "O Shahrazad, thou wouldst cause me to renounce my kingdom and thou makest me repent of having slain so many women and maidens" (III: 129).

Preceding the three hermit stories are two nested stories that focus on human violence toward animals: the "Tale of the Duck and the Peacock" and the "Tale of the Birds and Beasts and the Carpenter" (told by the duck), on the 146th and the 147th nights. The second one, while "indisputably a fable",[38] stands out by its sophistication, and the fact that its animal characters are not just allegorical stand-ins for human types conveying a political moral. It is in fact a condensed and simplified version of a story collected in the tenth-century Encyclopedia of the Brethren of Purity, *The Case of the Animals Versus Man Before the King of the Jinn*, which denounces "man's overreaching, oppression, and injustice against the creatures that serve him—the beasts and cattle—and his heedless, impious thanklessness for the blessings for which he should be grateful".[39] In this story, itself an adaptation of a fable of Buddhist origin,[40]

---

[37] Ballaster (2005b: 4); see also Lefkowitz 18–19.

[38] Irwin (1992: 50).

[39] *The Case of the Animals* (2009: 65) (Prologue). On the reception, popularity, and numerous translations of the story in Europe and Asia, see the introduction, especially 3–4.

[40] Irwin (2004: 252).

the animals bring a lawsuit to the court of the Jinn against Man; they complain of horrific abuse while Man argues that he is entitled to use animals as he pleases, since they are his slaves.

In the context of Shahrazad's story-telling, this "ecological fable"[41] is repurposed as a thinly veiled criticism of Shahryar's despotism. In the *Nights'* version of the story, the animals' poignant tale of human cruelty mirrors the case laid out before the king of the Jinn in the Epistle[42]: but the lawsuit and the judge have disappeared; instead the story focuses on the animals' desperate attempts to escape violence, first by a courageous but failed political rebellion, then by a withdrawal from society. Led by the lion, the animals form an alliance against Man, but the noble lion is no match for his treachery, as Man tricks the lion into a cage and sets it on fire. A typical fable moral (trickery wins over strength) here serves to illustrate a lesson about man's tyranny over animals. It is also a bitter lesson about political failure. The same is true about the framing story in which it is embedded: the duck (having just witnessed the lion's horrific end) seeks refuge from this traumatic experience on an island with the peacocks, far from Man; all is well for a while, but their utopian community is short-lived as sailors eventually arrive at the island and kill the duck.[43]

Recurring themes throughout these interlocking fables are the violence of the powerful over the powerless, and the desire to withdraw to an island: these animals, wishing to sever ties to a tainted world, are renouncers too. Capital lessons are being taught to the king in these pivotal nights. Most crucially, the animals' suffering at the hands of Man evokes that endured by the king's subjects. The stories chastise Shahryar for his bad stewardship: he has lain waste his own kingdom, wantonly

---

[41] Ibid. On the insertion of this animal fable (which was not part of the original core of the *Nights*) into later editions (in particular Calcutta II, the basis for Burton's translation), see Irwin (1992: 49–50).

[42] A recent children's edition of this story adapted the ending to better fit contemporary sensibilities: instead of animals remaining subject to men as in the original (albeit with the implicit caveat that all creatures are accountable to God), the animals win the case: the king of the Jinn orders men to change their destructive ways and behave responsibly toward nature (*The Animals' Lawsuit Against Humanity* 2005).

[43] A secondary theme in these stories is the importance of prayer: animals are blessed if they pray (III: 126), and killed if they don't (III: 125, 131). Shahryar, who sometimes forgets to say his prayers before falling asleep (III: 114, Note 1), takes notice, and thanks Shahrazad for her lesson (III: 132). Thus the fables teach the king a double lesson: political (his duty toward his subjects) and religious (his duty toward God).

killing women of childbearing age. By contrast, the shepherd–hermit characters carefully tending their animals offer an example that the king should follow.[44]

A repentant Shahryar expresses a fleeting desire to "renounce [his] kingdom" for a hermit's life, but this would be the wrong ending for a book so preoccupied with the here and now of power. Thus the hermits' rejection of women and society also offers the king an example that he should *not* follow, for fear of destroying the kingdom in another way. From the hermit stories, the king will learn not how to be a hermit, but how to be a good king, equally committed to his duty toward his subjects and the preservation of royal lineage and social integrity. Here the lesson taught Shahryar unexpectedly reconnects with its distant Buddhist origin: a trace of the conflict at the heart of Buddhism—the choice between a king's life and a hermit's life—still remains in its Arabic rewriting.[45]

Renunciation stories told in the secluded space-time of the *Nights* (whose realm is the night, the harem, the talking cure, the "nocturnal poetics", to quote Ghazoul's memorable title) paradoxically bring about the king's exemplary return to a regenerated social order, by way of the eremitic experiment.[46] The detour by the margins is a necessary part of the journey back to the center.[47] The night allotted for storytelling, and

---

[44]The shepherd trope is widespread across cultures: in the Epistle of the Animals the king is described as caregiver and shepherd (152, 270), echoing Diogenes's political distinction between a shepherd and a butcher. A good king, Diogenes told Alexander, should be like a shepherd, whose role "is simply to oversee, guard, and protect flocks, not, by heavens, to slaughter, butcher, and skin them... There is a world of difference between the functions of butcher and shepherd, practically the same as between monarchy and tyranny" (Dio Chrysostom 189).

[45]Aśvaghoṣa xxxiii–xlii. Further back still, it echoes the Indian classical tradition's theme of asceticism as a necessary phase to be overcome: Milanetti 285–291.

[46]Perhaps this is why Burton chose as his epigraph for his version of the *1001 Nights* a quote from the *Decameron* ("Niuna corrotta mente intese mai sanamente parole"), which features on the first page of his translation along with the picture of the labyrinth, and which he translated by the equivalent proverb "To the Pure All Things Are Pure" (III: 6). In the *Decameron*, the plague is both cause and metaphor of the societal breakdown, while the temporary retreat of the youthful characters to country villas, away from the diseased city-state, allows them playfully to transition back to its reformed version.

[47]On the hermit's shift from seclusion to engagement, see Ware in Wimbush and Valantasis 4–6. The ironic observation that "those who have chosen to live outside society have always been eagerly sought out for advice on how to live within it" forms the starting point of Peter France's *Hermits* (France xiii).

the night allotted for leaving the palace and relinquishing power mirror each other. Whether "real" (Harun al-Rashid living as a commoner for a night) or "fictional" (Shahryar vicariously experiencing his subjects' predicament), the storytelling strategy enacts the circuitous return of the reformed king to what, from his kingdom, has survived and is poised to begin anew.

A continuous preoccupation runs through these texts: the enduring dream of healing the polis through storytelling. Whether tales to entertain an Oriental despot, fables to awaken princely dunces, or words of wisdom to enlighten an emperor (the Western philosophical counterpart), stories enact the intellectual's perennial fantasy of doing things with words.

5   ASIATIC *PARRHESIA*

That's a slave's life—to be forbidden to speak one's mind. (Euripides, *The Phoenician Women*)[48]

The political efficiency of speech, the ascetic's power to convert the king, are bound up with the larger problem of speaking truth to power. The Greek notion of *parrhesia* (truth-telling) was the focus of Michel Foucault's late lectures.[49] Despite the different political and cultural contexts—Greek democracy vs. Eastern monarchy—his analysis is relevant to the present discussion. Foucault tied the concept of *parrhesia* to Greek political philosophy and the Athenian democracy, defining it as the free, direct, and public expression of political criticism by citizens equal in the eyes of the law. Speaking truth to power was "a right and a privilege which was part of the well-born, honorable citizen's existence, giving him access to political life understood as the possibility of giving one's view and thereby contributing to collective decisions".[50] Conversely, disenfranchised members of

---

[48] Euripides 248.

[49] From his lectures at the Collège de France in Paris to his last lecture series, delivered at UC Berkeley in 1983 and later published under the title *The Courage of Truth*: Foucault (2012).

[50] Foucault (2012: 34). Foucault also acknowledges the fundamental ambiguity of *parrhesia*, which led Plato and Aristotle to view democracy and *parrhesia* as incompatible, since democracy does not prevent demagogues from abusing *parrhesia* to spread lies and flatter the people. On the link between *parrhesia* and democracy, see also Dyrberg 78–81.

society (women, foreigners, or slaves) could not say what they thought. In Euripides' tragedy *The Phoenician Women*, Jocasta commiserated with her son Polyneices's experience as an exile deprived of the parrhesiastic right: "That's a slave's life—to be forbidden to speak one's mind".[51]

As democracy later gave way to "another type of political structure" (monarchy or tyranny), *parrhesia* relocated within the relationship between "the Prince and his counselor", which takes place no longer in the assembly but in the privacy of the prince's court (57). Although tyranny can make *parrhesia* difficult or dangerous—that tyranny generates silence or flattery is a commonplace throughout Greek literature[52]—it is nevertheless possible for a wise adviser to influence the tyrant, thus making the city's salvation conditional upon the prince's ethical formation (61–65).

An adviser speaking truth to the king's power seems much closer to Borges's dialogues of king and ascetic. Yet, with an Asiatic despot, direct truth-telling may not be possible.[53] As a fictional incarnation of the type, Shahryar is surrounded by slaves rather than citizens, his own wife being no exception. Under these circumstances, the only way of speaking truth to power is the slave's roundabout storytelling strategy. Not coincidentally, legend has it that Aesop the fabulist was a slave. Fables that entertain the despot while attempting to admonish him in metaphorical ways can therefore be understood as the East's version of *parrhesia*, "an important vehicle for frank speech in non-democratic" settings.[54] The fables of *Kalila wa-Dimna* qualify as (indirect) *parrhesia* within "an Arabic rhetorical tradition of scholars who articulate their political perspectives in their re-telling of stories".[55]

---

[51] Quoted in Foucault (2012: 53, Note 2).

[52] Foucault (2012: 59).

[53] Ancient anecdotes staging a dialogue (and a stern lesson) between a king and a wise advisor often make the king Oriental and the advisor Greek: for example, in Herodotus's *Histories*, the dialogue between the Lydian king Croesus and Solon the Athenian law-giver, or the dialogue between the Persian king Xerxes and the Spartan Demaratus (Herodotus 13–14; 449–450). On "Asiatic despotism" as an Orientalist type theorized by Western political philosophy since Aristotle, see Grosrichard 3–25.

[54] London 191.

[55] London 193. She further stresses the influence of the fables on later unorthodox writings such as the Epistles of the Brethren of Purity, whose "Case of the Animals" found its way into the Calcutta II edition of the *Nights*, as we saw. The fables' pedagogical purpose is made clearer still with Al Muqaffa's insertion of a tale of Buddhist origin, "The King and his eight dreams", which features a courageous and outspoken adviser (London 197).

Scheherazade is an Eastern *parrhesiastes*, a slave-adviser bold enough to speak truth to power—using "tales as a covert means of instructing a prince".[56] To influence the course of political action, she needs much more than a handful of fables: oceans of stories, *1001 Nights* of stories, are needed to reform the bloodthirsty Shahryar. Listening to her, the king briefly contemplates the ascetic life. This intention is short-lived, fortunately (or else there would be a power vacuum in the kingdom), but he has been reformed by his long dialogue with his wife-adviser. Life can finally go on. But what if the king were to take the other road at the fork, and leave his palace for good?

6   THE OTHERWORLDLY VARIANT: RADICAL RENUNCIATION AND THE ASCETIC IMPERATIVE

At the close of the book, the sultan is secured in his position of power and safely reinserted within the bounds of society, having left the palace only vicariously. But in Egyptian novelist Naguib Mahfouz's reworking of the tales, *Arabian Nights and Days*, abdicate is exactly what his twentieth-century namesake does. Crushed by the guilt of his crimes and convinced that all worldly power is irredeemably corrupt, at the end of the storytelling, Mahfouz's Shahriyar leaves his palace to become a wandering beggar: "He abandoned throne and glory, woman and child. He deposed himself, defeated before his heart's revolt at a time when his people had forgotten his past misdeeds. His education had required a considerable time... He left his palace at night, wearing a cloak and carrying a stick and giving himself over to fate".[57]

Several details (cloak, stick, woman and child) point to a Buddha-like model for the king's behavior: although Mahfouz's modern-day Shahriyar is cured of his murderous folly, he can no longer bear his royal status. Like king Milinda donning the yellow robe, his renunciation is definitive. However, renunciation leads him not to peaceful illumination but to bitter mourning, as he joins the daily line of weeping men who have squandered their chance of happiness, ending the novel—in somber contrast not only to the Buddhist renunciation story, but to the optimistic ending of the *1001 Nights*—on a note of despair.

[56] Ballaster (2005a: 348).

[57] Mahfouz 222.

In the otherworldly version of the king-and-ascetic dialogue, the radical outcome is definitive renunciation, brought about by a catastrophic sense of emptiness. This emptiness gnawing at the heart of absolute power and threatening to dismantle societal structures is the subject of Geoffrey Galt Harpham's seminal book, *The Ascetic Imperative in Culture and Criticism.* In the renunciatory spirit of early Christianity, giving up worldly power constituted the ultimate value.[58] Thus in the Christian version of the Buddha story, the hermit Barlaam tells a sequence of fables that persuade the young prince Josaphat to abdicate.[59] Although Harpham's corpus is centered on early Christianity, his argument is relevant in this broader context because he views asceticism as transcending cultural boundaries. While he acknowledges asceticism as a counter-cultural force, he argues that it is also, paradoxically, a necessary part of culture-building, "a primary transcultural structuring force".[60] Despite the "radically anti-cultural forms" their practices took—the isolation, the self-deprivations, the self-loathing "entirely incompatible with communal life or the family structure"—early Christian ascetics, he argues, are nevertheless the ones who brought "the Book to the Desert", serving as "apostles of a textual culture" (xii) in the process. Witness the legend of Anthony, who initially presented himself as a voluntary illiterate and an enemy of literacy, but who, in later iconography, became a saint of the book, commonly pictured reading.[61] The literary dimension of asceticism is where Harpham's argument intersects Borges's interest in the formation and circulation of legends. Asceticism propagated itself through "legends"—lives of ascetics read, retold and imitated. Bishop Athanasius's fourth-century *Life of Anthony,* "the master text of Western asceticism" offered Anthony's life in the desert as an exemplary model to imitate: imitation was the heart of ascetic practice, anchoring converts in "a community of imitation" originating in the imitation of Jesus Christ himself.[62] Ascetic narratives formed imitative chains: reading

---

[58] Almond (1987: 393).

[59] Voragine 744–752; on the power of stories in hagiography, see Jouanno 61–76.

[60] Harpham (1987: xiii). This central thesis of Harpham's book can be traced back to Durkheim, whose *Elementary forms of religious life* argued that asceticism is a necessary part of every religion and culture: Wimbush and Valantasis xxvi.

[61] More on the Anthony story in Chapter 3.

[62] Harpham (1987: 3, xiv).

about the ascetic exploits of saints triggered a decision to imitate them and renounce the world.[63]

The king's desire to leave his palace and become a hermit can now be revisited within this broader conversion framework. Harpham lays out the stacked narratives in Augustine's *Confessions* that lead Augustine and friends to embrace an ascetic Christian life in imitation of life-stories read or heard.[64] Ultimately Augustine's autobiography itself becomes part of the chain, "proposing a species of imitation with the power to convert, to bind the life of the reader into its own pattern" (96).[65] This power of ascetic stories to generate imitative action—to bind lives into legend—correlates with the dynamics of Borges's "legends" of renunciation, which, because they are simplified versions of biographical reality (true in their essentials, if erroneous in particulars), can easily migrate among individuals. Stories spawn other stories and lives reproduce other lives in a long chain, purified of individuality. The imitative chain of renunciation dovetails with the Borgesian view of literature as a chain of variations on a basic legendary plot, which in turn relies on the foundational Borgesian equation between living and reading.

7   VICTORIAN RENOUNCERS

At the end of the 19th century Oscar Wilde proposed a variation: The happy prince dies in the seclusion of the palace, without having discovered sorrow, but his posthumous effigy discerns it from atop his pedestal. (*SNF* 374)

The allusion to Oscar Wilde's "The Happy Prince", the last variation on the Renunciation archetype listed in the essay "Forms of a Legend", provides an unexpectedly childish ending to the long list of erudite references. Given the political significance of renouncer stories, we may find the presence of a Victorian children's story incongruous. Why does Borges bring up "The Happy Prince", giving it prominence as the final example in his essay? The intensity of the political context (Borges's clash with Peronist authoritarianism in the Buddha years) suggests that there is

---

[63] Articulating this principle, Josaphat applies Barlaam's stories to his own case: "Josaphat said: 'I see myself in that story, and I think you were really talking about me'" (Voragine 748).

[64] Harpham (1987: 95–96).

[65] Harpham (1987: 96).

more at stake than mischievous irony from a writer who refused to take himself too seriously. Indeed the playfulness might be one side of the coin, the other being political anxiety. "The Happy Prince", I propose, particularly when cross-read with Kipling's stories "The Miracle of Purun Bhagat" and *Kim*, allows some insight into Borges's ambiguous stance on the political dimension of the king-and-ascetic archetype, a confrontation made painfully personal by Argentine circumstances.

Wilde's story of a selfish prince, who was indifferent to his subjects' well-being during his lifetime but discovered their misery after his death and made belated amends by giving away the precious stones and gold of his statue to the poor, seems less out of place if we remember that "El Príncipe feliz" was the first text published by nine-year-old Borges.[66] This autobiographical allusion discreetly inserted into the essay on Buddhism suggests an intensely emotional investment in renunciation stories: it reaffirms the deeply personal nature of Borges's interest in Buddhism, and the importance of Victorian sources both scholarly and fictional. It also shows how Borges's own take on this tradition departs significantly from the Victorian model.

The popular fairy story by Oscar Wilde (a writer Borges admired)[67] provides an example of a typical Victorian reworking of the Buddha legend into an educational message of social ethics. The Happy Prince's posthumous conversion is to active philanthropy, as he exhibits a new concern for his subjects' "suffering" and "misery" and renounces his riches for them.[68] But Borges's plot summary appears to overlook the obvious social message of the story, focusing instead on its spiritual and metaphysical dimensions: what the prince discovers is not his subjects' "misery", but more abstractly "sorrow". Nor does Borges mention the prince's charitable actions. This de-emphasizes the people's poverty and realigns the prince's experience with the Buddha's.

In a similar vein Borges appears almost oblivious to the political tensions undergirding Kipling's renunciation stories for children, where the East–West polarity of active engagement vs. contemplative disengagement plays out with a clear didactic moral in favor of the former. Cross-read with Wilde's "Happy Prince", *Kim* (on which Borges commented

[66] See Chapter 1.

[67] In addition to an essay, "On Oscar Wilde" (314–316), we find no fewer than eight references to Wilde in *SNF* alone.

[68] Wilde 24.

on several occasions) and "The Miracle of Purun Bhagat" enrich and complicate the political afterlife of the king-and-ascetic stories and Borges's paradoxical take on them. "The Miracle of Purun Bhagat", first published in 1894 and subsequently included in the *Second Jungle Book*, is, as Angus Wilson points out, a "curtain raiser" for the later novel *Kim* (despite the differences in religious contexts), since Kipling pays tribute to both the Eastern way of life and the Western code of action.[69] The story's hero, Sir Purun Dass, is a Westernized Indian official lionized by the Victorian colonial elite, who, at the height of his power, renounces "position, palace and power", takes up "the begging-bowl and ochre-coloured dress of a Sunnyasi or holy man",[70] and settles in an abandoned temple high above a Himalayan village. The climax comes when torrential rains threaten to engulf the village in a mudslide: abandoning contemplative withdrawal in favor of active engagement, the ascetic turns back into a king. "He was no longer a holy man, but Sir Purun Dass, K.C.I.E., Prime Minister of no small state, a man accustomed to command, going out to save life" (173). The irony here goes both ways, as Kipling's hero, having first renounced his Western persona to live the contemplative life of a Sunnyasi, later renounces the Eastern values of renunciation in favor of the Victorian ethics of philanthropic action. Despite their admiration for many ethical aspects of Eastern religions, Victorian Orientalists strongly disapproved of what they saw as these religions' condoning of fatalism, passivity, or selfishness; Kipling's children's stories offer a simplified fictionalization of the issue.[71] Happily, in "Purun Bhagat" as in the later *Kim*, despite the much harsher delineation of colonial power relations, this conflict is resolved. The titular "miracle" refers to the reconciliation of opposite values: Purun Bhagat, having died like a hero, is worshiped like a saint. *Kim*, which pairs a Tibetan Buddhist monk and an Irish boy in friendship and adventure, also sets up a polarity between Eastern and Western values—between engagement and renunciation—which culminates in their reconciliation.[72]

[69] See Angus Wilson 23–33.

[70] Kipling (2013: 164).

[71] On Victorian critique of Eastern ethics, see Philip C. Almond (1988: 111–117 and 141).

[72] On Kipling's knowledge of Buddhism and appreciation of renunciatory religions, see Edmund Wilson 57 and Green 271.

The Lama's failure to sever emotional ties to Kim,[73] miraculously, does not jeopardize his quest for freedom from the Wheel of Things: on the contrary, his human weakness endears him to his readers, ultimately ensuring that he finds his river and achieves salvation after all, while also looking out for Kim.

Borges, whose admiration for Kipling never wavered,[74] and who repeatedly dismissed Kipling's racist ideology as irrelevant to his artistry,[75] recast *Kim's* political reconciliation between East and West, between India and England, as the philosophical union of action and contemplation. In a late interview, Borges praised Kipling's masterful interweaving of the two main plotlines, Kim's thrilling destiny in the Great Game and the Lama's quiet destiny as a Buddhist monk, culminating in the salvation of both heroes, "one through a life of contemplation and the other through a life of action".[76] Downplaying, even ignoring the colonial predicament (having a white hero grow up as an Indian only to end up working as a spy for the colonial government, a circumstance on which numerous critics have remarked),[77] Borges focuses instead on the abstract nature of the dichotomy and its resolution. If Kipling saw no conflict between the Lama's quest and the boy-spy's destiny in the powerful colonial machine, as Edward Said persuasively argued,[78] Borges goes further still, to the point where his philosophical reading might almost be construed as a "misreading", in the Bloomian sense, of highly

---

[73] "What shall come to the boy if thou art dead?... I will return to my *chela*, lest he miss the way" (Kipling 1989: 337).

[74] Kipling was for Borges "a lifelong companion" (Weinberger, *SNF* 526), one of his most constant literary models, from his early childhood readings—the *Just-So Stories* and *Kim*—to the very late stories "that nobody read", to borrow Edmund Wilson's title (17–69). Borges praised Kipling very highly, comparing him favorably to Maupassant, James, Joyce, or Kafka (*SNF* 251; *CF* 345), and translating many of his stories, including "The Gate of the Thousand Sorrows", "In the House of Suddhoo", "The Finest Story in the World", as well as several of the "Just So Stories", in the *Revista Multicolor* (Kristal 2002: 34–35 and 39).

[75] See for instance *OC* IV: 327 and 377–378; *SNF* 250–251; Christ 266, and Borges 1981: 32.

[76] Borges (1981: 32).

[77] For instance Edmund Wilson 30, later incorporated and reassessed in Edward Said's celebrated essay, especially 145–149.

[78] Said 146.

political stories. Although his judgment was recorded eighty years after the novel's publication and a full generation after India's independence, he soars so high above historical circumstances that the singular complexities of Kipling's Indian story fade into an essential polarity of action-vs-contemplation.

* * *

The king-and-ascetic motif raises the politically charged questions of the power of the powerless, and the agency of the word, as this chapter has tried to show. Against this rich political tradition Borges's view from a great height seems, at first, oddly disengaged. However, it would be wrong to dismiss Borges's ostensibly apolitical reading of these Victorian variations on the king-and-ascetic polarity—his lack of attention to either the Happy Prince's philanthropy, or the imperialist conundrum at the heart of *Kim*—as evidence of overall political indifference (albeit consistent with his aestheticized reworking of the king-and-ascetic motif into a king-and-poet motif, which is the focus of Chapter 3: "*From Ascetic to Poet: Poetic Renunciation*"). Borges was far from blind to the political importance of the motif: if anything, the motif's ubiquitous presence, in its myriad variations, throughout his work, is ample proof to the contrary.

Perched atop his pedestal like an early Christian stylite, the Happy Prince (separated yet not disengaged from his kingdom's tribulations) epitomizes Borges's discomfort with the role of public intellectual that he took on reluctantly as Perón's authoritarian grip on Argentina tightened.[79] Perhaps the essay's concluding reference to Wilde's Victorian renouncer should be read as a confession of sorts—a nostagia, not unmixed with guilt, for the sheltered life in the garden and the library behind the palace walls, that Borges had lived in his youth.[80] A heightened sense of the writer's political responsibility, along with a feeling of powerlessness in the face of tyranny, contradictory impulses toward withdrawal into aesthetics and sacrificial resistance (the happy prince, after all, gives up his eyes): all these emotions entered into Borges's writing in the fifties. Wilde's Happy Prince, the childhood icon crowning the long

---

[79] On Borges's presidency of SADE and other forms of his anti-Peronist cultural and political resistance, see Williamson (2007, especially 279–288).

[80] According to his famous autobiographical statement Borges "grew up in a garden, behind a speared railing, and in a library of unlimited English books" (Prologue to *Evaristo Carriego*; see Introduction, Note 6).

series of renouncers, pointed to the characteristic dilemma of a writer for whom the pen-vs-sword debate, and the question "whether the writer might be able to cross the line from writing to deeds" had become painfully personal, while his "reflections on art at a time of acute political crisis"[81] pulled him upward to poetic and philosophical heights. From that pedestal he soared above the circumstantial context, yet also paradoxically he was in no way unaware of or detached from the suffering kingdom.

The Happy Prince's predicament symbolically captures Borges's position—ambiguous, paradoxical—in the recurring confrontation of art and politics. His insistence on the pattern's recurrence underscores its pervasiveness, its enduring relevance in space and time. Yet privileging pattern, symmetry and recognition, at the expense of singularity and circumstance, also ensures that political conflicts are represented in a timeless rather than a historically specific manner. Perhaps the very fact that he steers clear of direct political discourse (against the grain of much contemporary Latin American writing) makes Borges a good writer to think with, politically speaking. Ascetics (and animals) are also good to think with: their marginal status with regard to the polis gives them certain privileges, not unlike the privileges Borges's landmark essay "The Argentine Writer and Tradition" granted Argentines and other marginal writers in the cultural sphere. They also provide a sustainably serviceable pattern for the relationship of literature to power: as the form of the conflict recurs, circumstantial accidents are irrelevant, while the pattern itself remains endlessly applicable. So in the late story "Undr", from the 1975 *Book of Sand*, the conflict between the king and the wandering poet becomes abstract: the aging poet, returning to the country whose king had ordered him killed years earlier, is told, not that this particular king has died, but that "his name is no longer Gunnlaug (…) now his name is other".[82] Individual identities and circumstances are erased and transcended by the cyclical nature of tyranny; conversely, we are encouraged to read the Viking story as a palimpsest of, for example, Argentine history.[83]

---

[81] Williamson (2007: 284 and 296).

[82] *CF* 458.

[83] Fiddian proposes a similarly palimpsestic reading of "Theme of the Traitor and the Hero" (101).

The morphological approach places ideas, history, and politics under the gaze of eternity. Unlike an explicitly committed writer whose stories provide a platform for political views, and notwithstanding numerous apolitical statements in interviews, Borges, precisely because of the double-edged strategy of analogies, offers an effective template for thinking about politics.[84] The pull toward the timelessness of recurring patterns, while distancing the king-and-ascetic confrontation from any specifics of time and place, also marks the perennial confrontation between a king wielding power and an ascetic wielding truth both as a philosophical commonplace (as Hannah Arendt defines it in her essay on "Truth and Politics")[85] and an aesthetic archetype. For Arendt "the conflict between truth and politics arose out of two diametrically opposed ways of life", the philosopher's and the citizen's.[86] To this pair one can add the poet, whose craft lies in discerning and arranging patterns, in which the meaning of stories resides. Stories of ascetics converting kings may not convert kings, but they resonate powerfully in times of crisis. Perhaps they point to what was, for Arendt as for Borges and Blixen, the "necessity of thinking poetically in dark times".[87]

---

[84]This is Robin Fiddian's argument: Fiddian 175. Apostol (2013) makes a similar claim for Borges as "a luminous thinker" of postcolonial politics.

[85]Arendt (2006: 223). Arendt's essay postdates Borges's Buddha essays by over a decade.

[86]Arendt (2006: 22).

[87]Wilkinson 95.

CHAPTER 3

From Ascetic to Poet: Poetic Renunciation

Abstract This chapter analyzes the aesthetic variant of the renunciation archetype. In Borges's poet stories, the king-and-ascetic pair morphs into a king-and-poet pair, with renunciation serving an artistic goal. The discussion traces this aesthetic appropriation back to the ancient and Renaissance tradition of artists' lives, and explores ascetic conceptions of art from Romanticism and Symbolism to modern art's debt to Cynicism, focusing on Borges's poet stories and artist stories from the Borgesian hypertext (by Flaubert, Schwob, Yourcenar, and Yi Mun-yol), where renunciation is a requirement of the creative process.

Keywords Artist lives · Poet stories · Yourcenar · Yi Mun-yol · Schwob · Flaubert · Aesthetic asceticism · Romanticism · Symbolism · Cynicism

Governor of the province in which he had been born (…) he abandoned it all in order to compose a book and a labyrinth. He renounced the pleasures of oppression, justice, the populous marriage bed, banquets, and even erudition in order to sequester himself for thirteen years in the Pavilion of Limpid Solitude.

("The Garden of Forking Paths")[1]

[1] *CF* 124.

© The Author(s) 2019
D. Jullien, *Borges, Buddhism and World Literature*, Literatures of the Americas, https://doi.org/10.1007/978-3-030-04717-7_3

For Ts'ui Pen, ancestor of the unhappy narrator in "The Garden of Forking Paths", renouncing the world and embracing an ascetic lifestyle were aesthetic choices. Like the Buddha, he renounced a life of privilege and power. Unlike the Buddha, his commitment was to art rather than religion. More precisely, spiritual energy was redirected toward an artistic goal. "The Garden of Forking Paths" features a new subspecies: the artistic renouncer. For Ts'ui Pen, whose masterpiece was misunderstood and mocked by all, renunciation also meant renouncing artistic fame. Shifting from a political to a poetic angle, this chapter explores a new reading path: renunciation as part of a creative trajectory.

Borges's essays on Buddhism paved the way for an intensely creative period marked by a return to poetry and short forms, and a focus on artist parables, such as "The Maker", which gave its title to the eponymous 1960 collection. Losing his eyesight like Borges himself, the parable's unnamed hero abandoned his early life of action and sensation, instead turning inward to become "Homer". "Then he descended into his memory", yielding to what awaits him henceforth: "the rumor of the *Odysseys* and *Iliads* that it was his fate to sing" (*CF* 293). Borges's fictions took a similar self-reflective turn: in his signature "poet stories" the ascetic morphed into a poet. Looking beyond Borges, this chapter also explores narratives that redirect the ascetic imperative toward creativity. Flaubert's saint Anthony, Schwob's Crates, Yourcenar's Wang-Fo, Yi Mun-yol's Kim Sakkat, all renouncer stories that are also self-portraits, are here examined in a Borgesian web of interconnected narratives about artistic renunciation. Along the way, the analysis weaves together different interpretative threads: the ancient and Renaissance tradition of artist lives which conflated creative, heroic, and saintly qualities, Foucault's late work on asceticism, especially the guiding intuition that the ideals of ancient cynicism live on in aesthetic form, and more generally the idea that a current of renunciation runs through much of modern art.[2]

1   THE BUDDHA AND THE MAKER

How does the Buddha morph into the Maker? Borges's morphological writing strategy, which generates potentially innumerable plots from variations on a finite number of archetypes,[3] is clearly seen in the

[2] Recently illustrated by Ross Posnock.

[3] As Ronald Christ argued in his seminal study, allusion is the key to Borges's art: all plots, all characters are allusions to other plots, other characters: Christ 37.

three palace parables that span forty years of the writer's career. From the archetypal king-and-ascetic dialogue resulting in the king leaving his palace, Borges derives the variant "Parable of the Palace", in which the outcome of the encounter between the Yellow Emperor and the poet is loss of palace for the emperor and death for the poet. Accidents vary, but actions remain,[4] as does the outcome of the encounter. "No sooner, they say, had the poet uttered his poem than the palace disappeared, as though in a puff of smoke, wiped from the face of the earth by the final syllable" (*CF* 318).

The later story "The Mirror and the Mask",[5] restages the archetypal encounter in a legendary medieval Irish kingdom; the outcome again is loss of the palace for the king and death for the poet. Here, however, the ending returns closer to its Buddhist source: the poet is a wanderer, bard, and beggar rolled into one, while the king becomes "a beggar who wanders the roads of Ireland, which once was his kingdom" (*CF* 454). Both the revelatory plot and the renunciatory ending replay the Buddha's story and his fateful words: "From this day forward I have no realm or my realm is limitless, from this day forward my body does not belong to me or all the earth belongs to me".[6] In both stories, the poem is the vehicle of a secret so powerful that it annihilates the king's former life and the world that was his palace, in an instant of realization that coincides with dispossession.

"A king is a plenitude, an ascetic is or wants to be nothing" (*SNF* 382)[7]: at the heart of the morphological process is the principle of *coincidentia oppositorum* which implicitly allows the two adversaries to trade places, at least for a moment. In "Parable of the Palace" the Yellow Emperor accuses the poet of usurping his place: "'You have stolen my palace!' he cried, and the executioner's iron scythe mowed down the poet's life" (318). In "The Mirror and the Mask", king and poet recite the esoteric poem together, and are punished jointly for the same transgression: "the sin of having known Beauty, which is a gift forbidden mankind" (454). While the king's first two gifts to the poet, the

---

[4]Working similarly to Proppian "functions" (Propp 29).

[5]From the 1975 collection *The Book of Sand*.

[6]"From Someone to Nobody", *SNF* 343. I discuss this essay later in the context of the Romantics' cult of Shakespeare.

[7]The Poet's indifference to the luxuries displayed before him as the Emperor shows off his palace (*CF* 318) shows he is a variant of the ascetic paradigm.

mirror and the mask, point to the illusory nature of individual identity (a key idea of Buddhism and of Borges's creative universe), the third, the dagger, suggests interchangeable identities and joint "deaths"— physical for the poet, statutory for the king.[8]

The idea at the heart of an earlier parable, "The Two Kings and the Two Labyrinths", is once again reversible identities—*coincidentia oppositorum*—underscored by the title's symmetry. The two kings are mirror images of each other, and one labyrinth substitutes another. The ascetic king—the Arab king, the man of the desert—defeats the rich Babylonian king, who loses kingdom, palace, and life in the open labyrinth of the desert. Emptiness triumphs over plenitude, nothing over everything. Furthermore, the ascetic king is a poet: the "labyrinth" he promises the Babylonian king is a metaphorical one, with "no stairways to climb, nor doors to force, nor wearying galleries to wander through, nor walls to impede thy passage" (*CF* 263).

2   BORGESIAN POET STORIES, ARTIST LIVES,
AND *KÜNSTLERROMAN*

Transforming the king-and-ascetic pair into a king-and-poet pair, Borges's poet stories also continue an ancient tradition of artist lives. This analysis draws on Ernst Kris and Otto Kurz's classic study of artist legends, which reflects on the archetypal anecdotes that shaped artist biographies since Antiquity, from Pliny to Vasari and beyond, even down to the present.[9] Common to Borges's poet stories and the formulaic painter anecdotes[10] analyzed by Kris and Kurz are the heroization of the

---

[8] Underlining their "secret kinship", Alexander and Diogenes are said to have died on the same day (*SNF* 382). For a Jungian reading of the twin polarities, see Rowlandson 22.

[9] E. Kris and O. Kurz *Legend, Myth and Magic in the Image of the Artist* (revised edition 1979). As late as the eighteenth century, Elisabeth Vigée Lebrun recycled stock painter anecdotes in her own autobiography: once Marie-Antoinette knelt down to pick up her brushes for her (Vigée Lebrun I, 68). Another anecdote was recycled in Balzac's *Unknown Masterpiece*: to meet the emperor, the painter Mabuse, a drunkard but also a genius, wore a paper costume painted like damask, having drunk up the money for the real damask (Balzac 27). Some of Kris and Kurz's examples are drawn from Asian cultures: more on this later in the discussion of Yourcenar's painter story, "How Wang-Fo Was Saved".

[10] Although the authors focus on visual arts (3), their findings have much in common with our poet stories.

artist's biography and a magical view of the creative process. The artist is sometimes depicted as a god (or devil), a mystic, a saint or even a martyr of his art.[11] Stock narrative motifs provide a kind of "movable scenery" (32–33) for artist's lives, reflecting "a universal human response to the mysterious magic of image-making".[12] The Borgesian morphing of ascetic stories into poet stories is nourished by this mythical tradition of artist biographies, whose "fixed biographical themes" (11) overlap with both heroic biographies and hagiographies.[13] Particularly relevant to Borges's poet stories are stories that point to a magical equation of picture and depicted, posit equality between a king and an artist, or stress the mystical nature of the creative experience.

The plot of "The Mirror and the Mask" relies on the magical identity—not likeness—of model and representation: "The verses were strange. They were not a description of the battle, they were the battle" (*CF* 452). It also turns on the idea of the artistic experience as taboo: poet and king must atone for "the sin of having known Beauty, which is a gift forbidden mankind" (454). The outcome of the story rests on yet another magical belief, the "heroic posture of self-destruction"[14] binding the artist's life to his work, and its destruction to his death: "Of the poet, we know that he killed himself when he left the palace" (454). Finally, the double loss (of life and kingdom) resulting from the confrontation illustrates the formulaic equality between king and artist.

This ancient tradition of artist biography dovetails with the more recent genre of the *Künstlerroman*. Borges's poet stories can be read as late reworkings of Romantic genius stories,[15] albeit in a highly condensed form that eschews biographical circumstances customary to artist

---

[11] There is further evidence of this in the case of Flaubert's *Saint Anthony*: see below.

[12] Gombrich's introduction, Kris and Kurz xii. Stock motifs include the early revelation of talent, for instance the child artist drawing his sheep (24–38); the painted object mistaken for a real one (61–66); the artist so absorbed in his work that he forgets to eat or sleep (125–129); the king honoring the artist as an equal, for instance picking up his brush for him (40–41), the work of art coming to life (69–72), etc.

[13] If hagiographies often align themselves on heroic biographies, artist lives draw on both traditions: Kris and Kurz 32.

[14] Kris and Kurz 131.

[15] On Borges's reworking of the Romantic genius myth, in particular in the English and American context, see Christ 207–226.

novels, in favor of a focus on epiphanic moments. Borges's life stories, his poet stories included, hinge on an instant of conversion when sinner turns into saint, king into ascetic, man into poet.[16] The conversion of the nameless warrior into the Maker—"Homer"—is one such epiphany, dispensing with the flow of events that fill a life, and attaching itself instead to an aleph-like point of revelation. In "Parable of the Palace" and "The Mask and the Mirror" the poem is a magic spell of devastating power: in its brevity (a few lines or a single word), it can conjure up an entire palace, even an entire world,[17] but it can also annihilate the world,[18] and destroy the men who dare to utter it.[19]

3   POETS-AS-ASCETICS IN WORLD LITERATURE

These different traditions (the myth of the artist as magician, the Romantic genius cult, the Modernist focus on epiphany) share a view of renunciation as a creative principle, and of the artist as ascetic.[20] The aesthetic reworking of the renunciatory archetype opens the stories to self-reflectiveness, makes them stories about art. Looking beyond Borges, this section considers other stories in which asceticism is redirected toward art, with renunciation a prerequisite of creativity. In the following four artist stories (by Flaubert, Schwob, Yourcenar, Yi Munyol) I propose to read the signature combination of poetic asceticism and self-reflection in a Borgesian light.

---

[16] The biographical formula is summarized at the heart of "A Biography of Tadeo Isidoro Cruz (1829–1874)": "Any life, however long and complicated it may be, actually consists of *a single moment*—the moment when a man knows forever more who he is": *CF* 213.

[17] "What we do know... is that within the poem lay the entire enormous palace, whole and to the last detail" (318).

[18] "No sooner... had the poet uttered his poem than the palace disappeared, as though in a puff of smoke, wiped from the face of the earth by the final syllable" (318).

[19] "Unable to summon the courage to speak it again aloud, the poet and his king mouthed the poem, as though it were a secret supplication, or a blasphemy" (453).

[20] On the secular rearticulation of asceticism as a modern aesthetic principle, see also Harpham (1995: 357–358) and Krul 123–125.

4   J. L. BORGES, AUTHOR OF *THE TEMPTATION* OF *SAINT ANTHONY*

> He was the Adam of a new species: the man of letters as priest, ascetic, and almost martyr.
>
> (Borges, "Flaubert and his Exemplary Destiny")

Although he had little appreciation for "Flaubert's laborious *Salammbô*",[21] Borges was a brilliant reader of Flaubert, to whom he devoted several important essays. These span fifty years of his essayistic career, from the early Thirties to the posthumous publication of the *Biblioteca personal* in 1988. Borges discusses Flaubert's idea of stylistic perfection ("The Superstitious Ethics of the Reader", 1931), alludes to Flaubert's satirical *Dictionnaire des idées reçues* ("The Total Library", 1939), ponders Flaubert's role in Modernism's mystical conception of literature ("On the Cult of Books", 1951), compares Bouvard and Pécuchet to Don Quixote and other absurd heroes ("A Defense of *Bouvard and Pécuchet*", 1954). That same year, in the longest and richest of the Flaubert essays, Borges sketches a portrait of Flaubert as a high priest of literary modernism ("Flaubert and his Exemplary Destiny", 1954).[22] Flaubert's fiction and correspondence contributed equally to shaping some of Borges's key ideas. Moreover, one of his last texts was a prologue to Flaubert's baroque hermit's tale.

Borges's prologue to *The Temptation of Saint Anthony* was collected in the posthumous *Biblioteca personal*.[23] Remarkably, Borges chose the relatively obscure *Temptation* over the better-known realist novels. His characteristically laconic essay highlights two key themes: the centrality of *Saint Anthony* to the rest of Flaubert's fiction, and the importance of Anthony as a self-portrait. Borges recalls the disastrous reception of the first draft by Flaubert's friends, who advised him to burn and forget

---

[21] *SNF* 506.

[22] These essays (except the final one, the prologue to *The Temptation of Saint Anthony*) are all collected in *SNF*: "The superstitious ethics of the reader" 52–55; "The total library" 214–215; "On the cult of books" 358–362; "A defense of *Bouvard and Pécuchet*" 386–389; "Flaubert and his exemplary destiny" 389–393.

[23] "Gustave Flaubert, *Las tentaciones de san Antonio*", *Biblioteca personal, OC IV*: 597–598. Borges only lived to complete 64 of the 100 projected prologues.

it. Crushed, Flaubert went on to write the arch-realist novel *Madame Bovary*, humiliating and punishing the romantic in himself; but he could never forget *Saint Anthony*, the work of a lifetime,[24] and far from burning it, he rewrote it entirely and published it in 1874.[25] Borges intuitively grasped what contemporary critics have analyzed at length: that this strange tale was the heart of Flaubert's creative universe, and in some way the fountainhead for all the other works, including, paradoxically, the realist masterpieces on which Flaubert's fame rests.[26]

Anthony, Borges points out, is a self-portrait. "Saint Anthony is also Gustave Flaubert. In the ecstatic and splendid final pages the monk wants to be the universe, like Brahma or Walt Whitman".[27] Whitman, while unknown to Flaubert, was of course a foundational reference for Borges, whose early poetry owed much to the American poet's celebration of a cosmic self.[28] Recognizing the same yearning in Flaubert, Borges interpreted Anthony's final religious temptation as Flaubert's poetic experience, onto which he projected his own, filtered through Eastern philosophy, and Whitman. A complex mirroring process is at work in this prologue despite its brevity: we see Borges seeing himself in Flaubert as Flaubert saw himself in Anthony's cosmic desire to "be matter itself." (190).[29]

Anthony's final, ecstatic fusion with creation seems closer to an Eastern mystical experience (seen through the prism of Arnold's fusional dewdrop) than to an early Christian spiritual experience: Brahma and Buddha appear toward the end of the book among the saint's

---

[24] "L'œuvre de toute ma vie": letter to Mlle Leroyer de Chantepie, 5 June 1872, *Correspondance* VI: 385; quoted in Bollème 252.

[25] Borges seemed unaware that there were actually three successive versions of the *Saint Anthony*: the manuscript of 1849, the longest, read privately to his friends just before Flaubert's trip to the Orient; a second draft written in 1856, and the definitive, shorter version of 1874, written just before *Bouvard and Pécuchet* (Flaubert 1968: i–ii).

[26] Several important critical studies focus on the interaction between the successive versions of *Saint Anthony* and Flaubert's other fictions. See especially Bem, Séginger and Neiland.

[27] My translation. In the original: "San Antonio es también Gustave Flaubert. En las arrebatadas y espléndidas páginas terminales el monje quiere ser el universo, como Brahma o Walt Whitman" (598).

[28] On Whitman's significance for Borges, from the discovery of *Leaves of Grass* in adolescence, to the lifelong translation work, see Kristal (2002: 46–55).

[29] Flaubert (2001: 190).

hallucinations (122–125). The ending remains ambiguous: has Anthony successfully overcome the temptation, as the English translator, Lafcadio Hearn, asserted in his summary?[30] Or is the dawn breaking at the end of the book simply the beginning of a new cycle that will take the saint through the painful repetition of the same visions and struggles? Lafcadio Hearn, who began the translation around 1875 or 1876, would become an important cultural bridge between East and West at the turn of the twentieth century.[31] For Hearn, who had studied for the priesthood, then later moved to Japan and converted to Buddhism, Anthony's brush with Eastern mysticism, his dream of absorption in universal matter, naturally seemed a crowning achievement for the ascetic's quest and a triumphant ending for the book. Borges, here, is rather close to Hearn's optimistic, Orientalist reading, but with a caveat: the monk, he writes, "wants to be the universe"—whether or not he gets his wish, we don't know.

Flaubert's self-image, then, is crucial to Borges's reading of the *Temptation*, as it is to his (unabashedly idiosyncratic) selection of this particular title as the one Flaubert book in his ideal library. Of course, Flaubert's near-pathological propensity to identify with his characters is legendary.[32] But the *Temptation*, in Borges's reading, is where the drama of Flaubert's self-portrait as a renouncer unfolds. Through his hermit character, and in his letters, Flaubert cast himself as an Egyptian saint, an ascetic in the desert of literature, actively elaborating his persona as the "Hermit of Croisset" that critics would enthusiastically endorse.[33] At the same time, Flaubert's ascetic penchant merged with his attraction

---

[30]"The temptation has passed; Anthony kneels in prayer" (Lafcadio Hearn, "Argument", in Flaubert 2001: 6).

[31]After much traveling throughout Europe and America, Hearn (1850–1904) settled in Japan, married a Japanese woman, became a Japanese citizen under the name Koizumi Yakumo, making a living as a university professor and journalist and writing over a dozen books about his adopted country. He also converted to Buddhism. For a biographical sketch highlighting Hearn's intellectual affinities with Flaubert, see Marshall C. Olds's Foreword (Flaubert 2001: ix–xiv).

[32]On the circumstances in which Flaubert uttered his famous (or famously apocryphal) declaration "Madame Bovary c'est moi", see Leclerc (2014). Flaubert's sympathetic symptoms as he was writing the fictional scene of Emma Bovary's nervous breakdown, are graphically described in his letter to Louise Colet (*Correspondance* II: 483).

[33]On this obsessive self-fashioning as a saint Anthony of letters at the time of the first *Temptation*, see Séginger 14–19. In a letter to Maxime Du Camp Flaubert fantasizes himself as a "brahmin" and a "hermit" (*Correspondance* I: 263; quoted in Séginger 18).

for Eastern spirituality, expressed repeatedly in his correspondence.[34] His interest in Buddhism continued and deepened over the years, culminating in extensive reading at the time of the *Temptation*'s third version.[35]

Remarkably, Flaubert was absorbed in books on Buddhism (and obscure theological erudition) while France was convulsed by the Commune and the subsequent repression. His disaffection for politics, a striking departure from fellow artists' humanitarian concerns, is obvious both in his fiction and his correspondence with George Sand, where he expressed his "immense disgust" for his contemporaries, adding that he spent the summer working on *Saint Anthony* and studying Buddhism.[36] His fierce ascetic, who fights off political ambition as one of the devil's most insidious temptations, embodies this anti-political stance. The second sequence of temptations reverses the paradigmatic king-and-ascetic encounter: Anthony hallucinates meeting emperor Constantine, who, far from being converted to the ascetic's life, crowns the saint and makes him his adviser. Anthony, drunk with power, revels in the humiliation of his enemies, the Fathers of the Council of Nicaea.[37] Politics as a temptation that the writer should be wary of: perhaps Borges, writing his late prologue in a time of chaos and violence in Argentina, sympathized with Flaubert's bitter aversion to politics?

Ultimately, it was the metatextual dimension of the *Temptation*—the portrait of the artist as ascetic—that captured Borges's imagination. Flaubert's "exemplary destiny" (the title of Borges's richest Flaubert essay) was to make literature into a new kind of religion. "He was the Adam of a new species: the man of letters as priest, ascetic, and almost martyr" (*SNF* 390). The Flaubert essays written in the early fifties (the Buddha years)[38] make the point repeatedly: Flaubert's cult of literature paved the way for

---

[34] Flaubert studies Buddhism, quotes the *Baghavad-Gita*, extols solitude and renunciation to attachments: *Correspondance* I: 263; Séginger 53.

[35] In 1871 Flaubert wrote to Frédéric Baudry, a philologist and childhood friend, that he was reading *Lalitavistara*, and desired to know more about its theology. He also mentioned that he had read Jules Barthélémy St Hilaire's two books on Buddhism (*Du Bouddhisme*, 1855, and *Le Bouddha et sa religion*, 1862): Flaubert (1982: 186).

[36] See Flaubert (1922). Letter CXCI, 25 July 1871.

[37] Flaubert (2001: 32–33). Flaubert compared current political disputes to ancient theological debates: Brooks 24.

[38] "On the cult of books" appeared in 1951; both "A defense of *Bouvard and Pécuchet*" and "Flaubert and his exemplary destiny" appeared in 1954.

modernism. "This mystical concept, transferred to profane literature, would produce the unique destinies of Flaubert and Mallarmé, of Henry James and James Joyce".[39] Unfathomable and diverse as God, Flaubert created both realistic stories (*Madame Bovary, L'Education Sentimentale*) and the wildly anti-realistic *Salammbô, The Temptation of Saint Anthony* or for that matter *Bouvard and Pécuchet*, which, Borges claims, "looks back to the parables of Voltaire and Swift and the Orientals, and forward to those of Kafka" (389). This combination of religion of art and creative diversity confers a God-like status to Flaubert, whom Borges evidently reads in the retrospective glow of Joyce: Flaubert "wished to be absent from his books, or barely, invisibly, there, like God in his works" (393), a statement that echoes the famous Joycean line from the *Portrait*, itself an homage to Flaubert: "The artist, like the God of the creation, remains within or behind or beyond or above his handiwork, invisible, refined out of existence, indifferent, paring his fingernails".[40] As a consequence, Flaubert's significance lies less in his fictions than in the persona of the artist as mystic and renunciant he created: "None of Flaubert's creatures is as real as Flaubert. Those who claim that his *Correspondence* is his masterpiece can argue that those virile volumes contain the face of his destiny" (393).

Flaubert extended renunciation to literature itself, aspiring to cut his art off from the market entirely. "Why publish, in these abominable times?", he wrote to George Sand in 1872.[41] In fact, the refusal to publish became almost a prerequisite for artistic worth: this self-sacrificial conception of the writer's condition was already expressed by a much younger Flaubert—equally consumed by literary ambition and by self-doubt—in a letter to Louise Colet, at the time of the *Temptation's* first draft.[42]

Borges, however, displayed a certain ironic skepticism toward this austere artistic ideal, criticizing Flaubert's literary martyrdom as essentially misguided, and his cult of stylistic perfection as "superstition":

[39] "On the cult of books", *SNF* 360. The same idea is repeated almost word for word in the 1954 essay (*SNF* 393). Hence Flaubert's name is linked both to realism and to its destruction: Flaubert, who forged the realist novel with *Madame Bovary*, "was also the first to shatter it", leading to James Joyce and the novel's "magnificent death" (*SNF* 389).

[40] Joyce 194–195.

[41] Flaubert (1922): Letter CCXLV.

[42] "Je ne veux rien publier. C'est un parti pris. Un serment que je me suis fait à une époque solennelle de ma vie" (8–9/8/1846; quoted in Bollème 38 and Séginger 18). Some of Borges's late artist characters exhibit this heroic self-abnegation.

"The perfect page, the page in which no word can be altered without harm, is the most precarious of all... On the contrary, the page that becomes immortal can traverse the fire of typographical errors, approximate translations, and inattentive or erroneous readings without losing its soul in the process".[43] By contrast, Don Quixote's ghost is alive in any language, independent of its original style or its translations.[44] Ultimately, Flaubert's "exemplary destiny" provided Borges with a foil to one of his foundational aesthetic beliefs: while he admired Flaubert's artistic integrity,[45] his own literary ideal, formed early on and revisited in the critical years of the Buddha essays and the polemics against literary nationalism, severed the text radically and definitively from its national and linguistic origin and required the broad sweep of world literature. As uncompromising as Flaubert but championing the opposite cause, Borges linked a work's ability to endure, not to its verbal perfection, but to its ability to be adapted, transformed, reworded.

4.1   Libraries on Fire: Flaubert, Borges, Foucault and the Triangle of Interpretation

Reflecting on Borges's reading of Flaubert's *Saint Anthony*, we run into an unexpectedly Borgesian state of affairs: today, the relation between the two is mediated by a third reader-writer, Michel Foucault. Foucault's reading of Flaubert, in particular of the *Temptation*, has achieved canonical status, to the point where the recent English language edition of the book includes Foucault's essay as its introduction. For better or for worse, we now see Flaubert's *Temptation* through a Foucauldian lens: we read Anthony's visions as a series of book-induced hallucinations, and the book itself as a book about books.[46]

[43] "The Superstitious Ethics of the Reader", *SNF* 54. This early essay, dated 1931, shows the depth of Borges's familiarity with Flaubert's works, biography and correspondence, and proves that Borges's fundamental ideas were articulated very early on, and would only be refined or modulated in later years.

[44] In similar vein, the *Odyssey*, which Borges could only read in translation, was "an international bookstore of works in prose and verse" ("The Homeric Versions", *SNF* 70).

[45] "Flaubert and his Exemplary Destiny", *SNF* 392.

[46] The book itself, far from protecting Anthony from the devil, becomes the site of temptation (Flaubert 2001: xxx). Thus, opening the Bible at random, Anthony lands on a scene of animal slaughter from *Acts* X:11–13; another attempt leads him to the massacre of the Jews' enemies in the *Book of Esther* IX:1–16 (Flaubert 2001: 15–16). Anthony's hallucinations are "not the product of dreams and raptures, but a monument to meticulous erudition" (Flaubert 2001: xxv).

Departing radically from the historical, illiterate Anthony, Flaubert's ascetic, rather like saint Jerome, another desert hermit, is a saint of the book. As the ascetic withdraws into the book, Flaubert's text creates a new kind of fantastic, which does not refer to the outside world or even an inner world of the mind, but "is a phenomenon of the library" (xxvi). Foucault underlines the continuity between *The Temptation* and *Bouvard and Pécuchet*, whose protagonists withdraw from the world in order unquestioningly and disastrously to put into practice their gargantuan reading (xli).[47] For Foucault the new dawn at the end of the *Temptation* points not to the saint's victory but to the cyclical routine of temptation and prayer, anticipating the repetitive predicament of the hapless *bonshommes*, but also the Borgesian universe-as-library.

Saint Anthony, Foucault argues, paved the way for much of contemporary literature. "Flaubert produced the first literary work whose exclusive domain is that of books: following Flaubert, Mallarmé is able to write *Le Livre* and modern literature is activated—Joyce, Kafka, Pound, Borges. The library is on fire" (xxvii).[48] Here the Borgesian reading comes full circle, as Foucault includes Borges in the list of modernist writers for whom Flaubert was a key precursor: Foucault's reading of the *Temptation* as a proto-Borgesian text affects our reading of both Flaubert and Borges.[49] Foucault's Borgesian Flaubert exemplifies the reverse influence described in Borges's iconic essay "Kafka and his Precursors" (*SNF* 363–365). Onto Flaubert's *Temptation*, Foucault projected the Borgesian nightmare of an endless and chaotic library, as well as the notorious "Chinese encyclopedia" dreamed up in the 1942 essay "The Analytical Language of John Wilkins", which became a seminal inspiration for his ground-breaking

[47] On this kinship, see Bernheimer 65–78.

[48] Curiously, the translators, Donald F. Bouchard and Sherry Simon, left out Raymond Roussel, who was a key influence for Foucault, although admittedly a relatively obscure writer for English-speaking readers. In the original: "Après *Le Livre* de Mallarmé deviendra possible, puis Joyce, Roussel, Kafka, Pound, Borges" (Foucault 1983: 107).

[49] In fact, it seems likely that he has read closely Borges's essays on Flaubert, in particular "Defense of *Bouvard and Pécuchet*", which makes a case for the kinship between sainthood and stupidity. Borges quotes critic Emile Faguet's epigram, "*Bouvard and Pécuchet* is the story of a Faust who was also an idiot" (*SNF* 387), and recalls the long tradition of placing wisdom in the mouths of holy fools, madmen or idiots (*SNF* 388). The link, Foucault observes, runs throughout Flaubert's fiction, connecting Charles Bovary to Félicité, to Bouvard and Pécuchet, and to Anthony whose wish is to be annihilated in pure matter (Flaubert 2001: xliii).

Order of Things.[50] The intersecting and bifurcating paths of cross-readings lead unexpectedly back to Pierre Menard's invisible work: in this chamber of Foucauldian echoes, Borges becomes the author of *The Temptation of Saint Anthony*.

5   FIN-DE-SIÈCLE CYNICS: MARCEL SCHWOB'S CRATES, ARCH-RENOUNCER

I have no wife, no children, no governor's palace, but only the earth and sky and an old cloak. And what do I lack? Am I not without grief and fear, am I not free?

(Epictetus, III, xxii)[51]

The transformation of the illiterate desert ascetic into an impassioned reader tormented by book-induced hallucinations exemplified the Romantic transfer of spiritual truth to the aesthetic realm which also informed Flaubert's self-image as an ascetic. Marcel Schwob's hero is a different sort of ascetic. Crates, the third-century Greek cynic, although less famous than his mentor Diogenes, took renunciation even further than him. An arch-cynic, Crates scorned books and any kind of authority, endeavoring to live more like a dog than a man. Looking at Schwob's "Crates, Cynic" (*Imaginary Lives*, 1896) through the lens of Borges's renunciation stories enables us to explore the current of cynicism that flows through the modern tradition of artistic asceticism as analyzed by Foucault (and later, Sloterdijk).

The "Precursor" effect is at work here as well: today the name of Marcel Schwob, in particular his best-known book, *Imaginary Lives*, is closely linked to Borges. Borgesian scholarship has rekindled interest in the French Symbolist: new editions of his works carry prefaces by Borges, and both texts and interpretations are filtered by Borges.[52]

---

[50] "The Analytical language of John Wilkins", *SNF* 231. Foucault's preface to *The Order of Things* opens with an allusion to the impossible Chinese taxonomy of animals in the Borges piece (Foucault 1970: xv). On the Borges-Foucault intertext, see O'Sullivan 109–121.

[51] Quoted in *The Courage of Truth*: Foucault (2012: 171).

[52] The 1992 edition of *La Croisade des enfants* (*The Children's Crusade*) carries a preface by Borges. On the recent renewal of interest in Schwob, see Berg (2007).

Borges's first attempt at narrative, *Universal History of Infamy* (1935),[53] was partly modeled on *Imaginary Lives*, although Borges would be many years in acknowledging his debt.[54] Perhaps unsurprisingly, Borges in his last years was revisiting his beginnings: moving back to Geneva where so many formative literary experiences took place, Borges found himself returning to Schwob's works, read passionately as a teenager.[55] Over the course of a few months in 1918, the young Borges, newly proficient in French, devoured all the works by Schwob that he could find. His youthful admiration was later encouraged by his mentor Rafael Cansinos Asséns, who translated *Imaginary Lives* into Spanish.[56]

Affinities abound: like Borges, Schwob admired Stevenson (undertaking a deathbed pilgrimage to Stevenson's grave in Samoa in 1901)[57]; Walt Whitman and Schopenhauer.[58] Despite their physical limitations (continual illness for Schwob, near-blindness for Borges), or perhaps because of them, they shared a taste for adventurous tales and dangerous heroes—criminals, gangsters, pirates, street toughs—as well as a scholar and poet's interest in slang.[59] Like Borges, Schwob was a writer's writer, a man who had read all the books, who drew inspiration from erudition,

---

[53] Borges's original title is *Historia universal de la infamia*. Norman Thomas Di Giovanni translates "infamia" as "infamy" (Dutton, 1972), and Andrew Hurley as "iniquity" (*CF* 1). However, since "*Infamy*" retains the wordplay with "fame" or lack thereof (both in the case of the protagonists and of the author, who was still far from famous in 1935), I use the words "infamy" and "infamous" throughout this section.

[54] Schwob's intertext, especially *Le Roi au masque d'or*, was first pointed out by writer and translator Roger Caillois in his "Translator's postface" (Borges 1971). See Caillois (1973: 29–32) and Levine (1973: 24). The *Autobiographical Essay* of 1970 indirectly admitted the filiation: "En *Infamia* no quería repetir lo que hizo Marcel Schwob en sus *Vidas imaginarias*". See Zonana (2000: 675). Later still, Borges chose *Imaginary Lives* as one of his hundred favorite books in his *Personal Library*, acknowledging it as a source for *History of Infamy: OC* IV: 601.

[55] According to Bernès, Borges re-read Schwob and Remy de Gourmont just before his death: *OCP* I, 1484.

[56] *OCP* I, 1483–1484.

[57] Schwob (1990). On the Stevenson-Schwob intertext, see Kleingut de Abner 265–271.

[58] Kleingut de Abner 89, 137.

[59] Schwob published a study of slang and Villon; Borges was drawn to milongas and lunfardo.

as well as a polyglot, a translator and a cultural mediator.[60] Even the hypertextual posturing was similar, from Schwob's anxiously derivative rewriting of other texts to the young Borges's "shyness" which kept him from inventing his own stories.[61]

In 1933–1934, just before publishing his own "infamous" biographies, Borges translated several of Schwob's *Imaginary Lives*,[62] beginning with last of Schwob's collection, "Mssrs. Burke and Hare, assassins", the one that for him best implemented the concept of "imaginary life".[63] Brevity, focus on a small number of key events, mix of fact and fiction, creative departure from historical sources: all these features are common to Borges and Schwob.[64] In his prologue to *The Children's Crusade* Borges praised Schwob's imaginative freedom over "Flaubert's anxious archaeology".[65] Schwob's preface exonerated the biographer from the duty of truth: "As an art, biography is founded upon choice; truth need not be its preoccupation, for out of a chaos of human traits it can create".[66] *Imaginary Lives* paved the way for Borges's signature biographies, which he practiced both as a critic, composing "capsule biographies" of famous writers,[67] and as a fiction writer, eschewing duration and psychology. It would also allow him to reflect on the foundational notion of "legend", which kept equal distance from historical and fictional criteria.

---

[60] Schwob translated works by Stevenson, Oscar Wilde, De Quincey, DeFoe, among others (Lhermitte 32; Viegnes 244). On Schwob's passionate relationship to books, see Stead 29–49.

[61] "They are the irresponsible sport of a shy sort of man who could not bring himself to write short stories, and so amused himself by changing and distorting (sometimes without aesthetic justification) the stories of other men", Borges wrote in the Preface to the 1954 edition (*CF* 4). On hypertextuality and rewriting in Schwob, see Lhermitte, especially 25–144.

[62] "Los señores Burke y Hare (asesinos)", September 1933; "El Capitán Kid", October 1933; "La muerta que escuchó la queja de la hermana enamorada", December 1933; "El incendiario", January 1934; "Petronio no se abrió las venas", March 1934. All published in *Revista Multicolor*. García (2011).

[63] Levine (1973: 25).

[64] These features can be traced further back to Walter Pater's *Imaginary Portraits*, one of Schwob's main models: Salha (2015).

[65] *OC IV*: 156.

[66] Schwob (1924: 20).

[67] The "Capsule Biographies" were written in the late thirties, directly after the *Infamy* narratives, and published in the magazine *El Hogar*. A selection is included in *SNF* 153–173.

Schwob's *Imaginary Lives* were heavily indebted to artists' lives in the Vasari tradition. His life of Paolo Uccello, the central story in the volume, was directly adapted from Vasari's biography, and several more Imaginary Lives concerned artists.[68] Other lives followed the artist's life pattern, in particular the last biography, "Burke and Hare, assassins", on the notorious assassins who supplied Dr. Knox with fresh corpses for dissection. Schwob playfully distinguished two "periods" in their career, the "classical" period (indoor murders, preceded by whisky and conversation with the victims), and the "Romantic" period (outdoor murders in the foggy streets of Edinburgh). Burke, the mastermind, was troped throughout as a playwright[69] and a modern Scheherazade, with Hare acting as his Dinarzade.[70] Schwob's inspiration can be traced back to De Quincey's 1827 essay "On Murder Considered as one of the Fine Arts", translated by Schwob and equally admired by Borges. Schwob's gallows humor also fed Borges's enduring fascination for gangster mythology, whether Argentine outlaws or American criminals from Von Sternberg's films. It gave Borges a model of irony for his first collection of stories, which tightened even further the link between artist's and criminal's lives—his biographer's duty being to confer a measure of "fame" on these "infamous" characters.

Schwob's heroes all follow the characteristic model of artists' lives, as delineated by Kris and Kurz. Schwob's Uccello is even more of a hermit and a mystic than Vasari's.[71] Schwob's artists and criminals are all marginals,[72] but three especially so. In addition to Crates (on whom more below), two other renouncers live on the fringes of society, the medieval heretic Fra Dolcino, and the Latin novelist Petronius, author of the *Satyricon.*

---

[68] Lucretius, Petronius, Cecco Angiolieri, Gabriel Spenser, and Cyril Tourneur. Schwob owned a copy of Vasari's *Lives* in English translation: Lhermitte 110. On the Vasari-Schwob intertext, see Lhermitte 105–110. On the dialogue with Paul Valéry's essay on Da Vinci, see Jullien (1996: 263–275).

[69] On the artist-criminal comparison, and on the image of the biographer as counterfeiter, see Salha (2015) and Christ 129–130.

[70] On the sustained *1001 Nights* analogy, see Kleingut de Abner 163–168.

[71] Lhermitte 126.

[72] Rabaté analyzes the lives of marginals in the context of Decadent imagination (184). Kleingut de Abner connects Schwob's predilection for marginal protagonists both to Villon's celebration of low-lives in his slang ballads, and to the marginalization of Jews at the time of the Dreyfus Affair (33–43).

"Fra Dolcino, heretic" romanticizes the life of the thirteenth-century martyred leader of the Order of Apostles. Schwob's Fra Dolcino is a simple mystic. Initially inspired by the Franciscan movement, he took renunciatory practices even further, advocating poverty, communism, wandering, begging or stealing, a rejection of all rules or predication. For his defiance of the Catholic and feudal authorities, he was burned at the stake, along with his companion, a young noblewoman named Margherita, in 1307.[73] By including Fra Dolcino—an icon of marginality and rebellion in Italian political culture to this day—among his gallery of rogues and geniuses, Schwob offered a belated, ironic variation on the Romantic myth of the cursed artist.[74]

"Petronius" deliberately turned away from Tacitus's historical account, which had the novelist commit suicide after falling out of favor with emperor Nero.[75] Instead, Schwob's Petronius, bewitched by the adventurous lives of his own characters, leaves his luxurious home and comfortable existence for the thrills of slumming he had described in his famous *Satyricon*. As he wanders across the imperial underworld, begging, stealing, and cheating his way, he cascades from one indignity to the next. He is eventually murdered by a chance lover: "A drunken thug had sunk a wide blade in his neck while they were lying together on the stone of an abandoned grave in the open country".[76] In this parody of

[73] "Crates, Cynic" shares the motif of the young and beautiful patrician woman who falls in love and renounces everything to follow the ascetic's way of life to the bitter end. Schwob's portrayal differs significantly from historical accounts. According to those, he was of noble birth, highly educated, and he eventually adopted a violent view of religion, leading a guerilla-like existence in the hills of Piedmont, plundering villages and killing villagers in the name of saint Paul (Pierce 2012). By contrast, Schwob's Fra Dolcino is a hippie *avant la lettre*, a humble and gentle soul, naïvely attached to a childhood memory: "He asked that they should not be stripped, but burned in their white mantles, like the apostles on the lamp-shade in the refectory of the Franciscans" (114). On Schwob's use of Franciscan sources, see Fabre 217–219.

[74] Fra Dolcino and his martyred Order of Apostles became icons of the revolutionary left in Italy in the 1970s, celebrated by Nobel prize-winning playwright Dario Fo in his *Mistero Buffo*. Schwob's imaginary biography is also a key hypotext for Umberto Eco's *Name of the Rose*: Cornille 298.

[75] Tacitus 385–386. Emphasizing the story's sensationalism, Borges translated the title as "Petronius did not open his veins" (Kleingut de Abner 280).

[76] Schwob 93; translation modified.

ascetic renunciation, squalor retains a poetic lining (Proust's Charlus would remember this); the quixotic element (a man acting out a book) would inevitably endear him to a Borgesian reader.[77]

In "Crates, Cynic" Schwob closely follows his ancient source, third-century Greek biographer Diogenes Laertius's *Lives of Eminent Philosophers*,[78] retaining in particular the quixotic renunciation anecdote. By one account, Crates (365–ca 285 BCE) was born to a wealthy Theban family, and his decision to renounce his fortune was triggered by seeing a similar scene onstage: "One day, while attending a tragedy by Euripides... he saw Telephy, king of Mysias, dressed in beggar's rags with a basket in his hand. So Crates stood up on his feet there in the theater, declaring he would give the two hundred talents of his inheritance to all who wanted the money" (47).[79] Schwob also borrowed from Diogenes Laertius the beggar's sack-as-kingdom metaphor ("He called the sack his city, a city without parasites or courtesans... a fine storehouse of thyme, garlic, figs and bread for its king", 48), and his encounter with Alexander, "whom he considered merely as one with the spectators, acknowledging no difference between king and crowd" (50). Schwob's anecdotes about Crates's wife Hipparchia and his disciple Metrocles are also drawn from Diogenes Laertius. Hipparchia, a beautiful heiress, fell in love with Crates despite his ugliness and squalor, renouncing all to share his life. Metrocles, Hipparchia's brother, became his disciple after Crates rescued him from shame by demonstrating that *naturalia non sunt turpia*.[80]

---

[77] Another quixotic hero is Major Stede Bonnett, who becomes a pirate after reading too many piratical adventures: "Nearly every evening he called his servants together under a grain shed to read them stories of the great exploits achieved by the pirates of Hispaniola or Turtle Island" (235). In his prologue to *Imaginary Lives*, Borges compares Schwob himself to Don Quixote, the "enchanted reader" ("maravillado lector"): *OC IV*: 601.

[78] Book VI is devoted to Crates, with Chapters 6 and 7 devoted to his disciple Metrocles and his wife Hipparchia. Schwob's life of Empedocles is also based on Diogenes Laertius. Borges's claim that Schwob wrote about historical characters of whom almost nothing is known is not correct in this case: Zonana 680.

[79] Borrowed from Diogenes Laertius, VI, 5, 87.

[80] Ashamed of his pathological flatulency, Metrocles wanted to die. In order to comfort him, Crates ate a large quantity of lupins, then "broke wind in the presence of his disciple and asserted that nature subjected all men to the same evil (...) Then he farted some more, took Metrocles by the hand, and led him away". Translation mine. Lorimer Hammond censors this passage of Schwob's text, which is based on Diogenes Laertius, VI, 6, 94. On Diogenes's shamelessness, see Sloterdijk 167–169.

However, Schwob also deviated significantly from his ancient source, dramatically softening Crates's image from an abrasive, rude cynic in the manner of Diogenes to a gentle philanthropist. "Though he never took part in public affairs, he never criticized them. He launched no insults nor did he approve this trait in Diogenes... Crates was kind to men. He reproached them with nothing" (48–49). Ancient anecdotes about Crates's aggressive behavior were left out.[81] Schwob's hero is indifferent to political and religious affairs, to kings and gods, but tolerant of any human misery, a cynic willing to live like a dog rather than bite like a dog (51).

Likewise, Schwob profoundly transformed Hipparchia's character. Diogenes Laertius's Hipparchia was an outspoken feminist philosopher, boldly placing philosophy above wifely duties.[82] In stark contrast, Schwob's Hipparchia became a pagan saint: "Hipparchia was kind to the poor. Compassionate, she soothed the sick with her hands, cleansing their bloody wounds without repugnance... When nights were cold she and Crates slept close to other poor folk, sharing the warmth of their bodies. From the beasts they learned the wordless kindnesses of beasts" (52).[83] In Schwob's reworking of Diogenes Laertius, the voluntary suffering of renunciation aimed not at the philosophical practice of virtue, but at empathetic solidarity with other sufferers, in accordance with an ethics of pity that bridges pagan, Christian and Buddhist virtues across Schwob's texts.[84]

Crates's life at the bottom sharing scraps with dogs (53) literalizes the etymology of the word "cynic" and makes him both beast and god, mocking the Aristotelian golden mean of humanity.[85] It also signals his indifference to philosophical doctrine: philosophy in his case is a way of

---

[81] Crates beating relatives come to take him home, insulting prostitutes, humiliating Alexander, or abusing fellow Athenians: Diogenes Laertius, VI, 5, 88–92.

[82] Diogenes Laertius VI, 7, 98.

[83] On hagiography and personal myth in Schwob's renunciant characters, see Lhermitte 328.

[84] Hipparchia resembles the saintly heroines of Schwob's *Livre de Monelle*, while Crates, a Greek Cynic turned sacrificial saint, recalls the Indian king in the earlier story "Le Dom" (published in *Cœur double* in 1891) who renounces his palace and his family, Buddha-like, for an ascetic life of unimaginable squalor and pain: Fabre (2006: 37–52).

[85] Lhermitte 493.

life, not a textual corpus or a theoretical system. This is true of Cynics in general: the Cynic's *bios*, the stripping bare of existence in order to reach the truth, is his only and sufficient work, as Foucault stressed in his final writings.[86] The idea endured from Antiquity to the present, traversing the realms of religion, politics, and art: *The Courage of Truth* ends with a historical meditation that traces the absorption of ancient cynicism into Christian values, Revolutionary ethics, and the practice of modern art. Schwob's syncretic hagiography of Crates echoes the martyr Peregrinus, "a Cynic who passed through Christianity, or a Christian who [became] a Cynic".[87] The Middle Ages saw recurring revivals of the Cynic ideal of nudity in Christian form—the mendicant orders, the Franciscan movement, the many heresies—and a contemporary resurgence can be detected in the revolutionary life, from nihilism to anarchism or terrorism.[88]

Cynicism, Foucault claims, endured in modern art, which became "the vehicle of the Cynic mode of being, of the principle of connecting style of life and manifestation of the truth" (2012: 187). Modern art's relation to reality is "no longer one of ornamentation, or imitation, but one of laying bare, exposure, stripping, excavation, and violent reduction of existence to its basics"; the artist's life isn't only "the condition of the work of art", but even "work of art itself" (2012: 188). Schwob's renunciant hero—a Greek Cynic for Fin-de-siècle France, a small figure in a web of Vasari-inspired lives—is one such cynic-cum-heretic poised on the cusp of late Romanticism.

6   RENUNCIATION AS VANISHING ACT: MARGUERITE YOURCENAR'S WANG-FO

One of the first major texts by the famously reclusive writer was the story of a renunciant painter, "How Wang-Fo Was Saved". The last text Yourcenar wrote was an essay on Borges in 1987, shortly after his death

---

[86] Crates's doctrinal legacy boils down to a handful of sayings, passed down in anecdotal form; the ancient Cynic tradition in general contained very few texts and a rudimentary doctrinal framework: Foucault (2012: 202).

[87] Foucault (2012: 181). On Peregrinus and the bridge between ancient Cynics and early Christian ascetics, see also France 18–19.

[88] Foucault (2012: 182–185).

and before her own.[89] She had discovered Borges's work through her friend Silvia Baron Supervielle, translator of Borges into French. Borges and Yourcenar formed an intense literary friendship in their old age, conducted largely in letters and telephone calls. Yourcenar visited the dying writer in Geneva in June 1986.[90]

Similarities between the two writers abound. Both lived very long lives that spanned almost the entire century. Both had unconventional educations, marked by solitude, extensive travel, multilingualism, and a strong Classical focus. Both writers were important cultural mediators and translators.[91] Both writers enjoyed a nurturing, almost symbiotic relationship with their fathers, who transferred onto their progeny their own literary dreams.[92] Both writers also shared a deep anxiety toward their early writings, even desiring to destroy them.[93] On the flip side, both writers' key motifs were formed very early on, as a generative core that successive books would rework and modulate.[94] Published in 1951, *Memoirs of Hadrian*, which made Yourcenar famous overnight, was begun in her late twenties.

Both writers were powerfully attracted to Eastern philosophies, especially Buddhism, Hinduism, and (in Yourcenar's case) Daoism.[95] Echoing Borges's taste for pseudo-Oriental stories ("The Approach to Al-Mutasim", "The Garden of Forking Paths", "Parable of the Palace", etc.),[96] Yourcenar's collection of stories from the Thirties was published under the title *Nouvelles orientales (Oriental Tales)*, an homage to Arthur

---

[89] "Borges ou le voyant" (Borges, or the seer), first given as a lecture at Harvard on 14 October 1987, collected and published posthumously in *En pèlerin et en étranger. Essais* (Yourcenar 1989: 233–261).

[90] Halley 185–189.

[91] Yourcenar translated from English, ancient and modern Greek, and Japanese: Barbier 12.

[92] Yourcenar's father, Michel de Crayencour, sponsored the publication of her first two books of poetry, helped her invent her anagrammatic pen name, and gave her his own abandoned novel to rewrite (Savigneau 53, 59–60). On Borges's complex relationship to his father's literary ambitions, in particular to the novel *El caudillo*, which he also contemplated rewriting, see Rodríguez Monegal 79–84.

[93] On Yourcenar's censorship, destruction or rewriting of early texts, see Yourcenar (1984: 188), Allamand 169 and Vázquez de Parga 99.

[94] As examples of generative motifs Golieth lists Borges's epiphanic experience "Feeling in Death" (*SNF* 324) and Yourcenar's quasi-mythical lost draft *Remous* (on which also Savigneau 62–63): 173–174.

[95] Yourcenar (1984: 202).

[96] Vásquez de Parga 102.

de Gobineau's 1876 *Nouvelles asiatiques* and to the rich tradition of Orientalist fiction. Orientalist amalgamation prevails in these early tales, which span a fantasy "Orient" from Greece to Serbia and Japan. The opening story, "How Wang-Fo Was Saved", is "based on a Taoist fable of ancient China", Yourcenar claimed.[97] Spurious source attributions are another feature Yourcenar shared with the young, insecure author of *A Universal History of Infamy*, who omitted the key intertext (Schwob) from his preface.[98] In reality, a much more direct source for the story is Lafcadio Hearn's "Story of Kwashin Koji", in which the painted boat magically rescues the painter from the evil emperor.[99] Chinese elements are there too, of course. The well-known legend of Ma Liang's magic paintbrush finds its way into the story: "It was murmured that Wang-Fo had the power to bring his paintings to life by adding a last touch of color to their eyes. Farmers would come and beg him to paint a watchdog, and the lords would ask him for portraits of their best warriors" (7).[100]

"Wang-Fo" is also an artist legend in the Vasari tradition. *Oriental Tales* is framed by two painter stories, "How Wang-Fo Was Saved" and "The Sadness of Cornelius Berg".[101] Wang-Fo's demiurgic ability to make painted creatures come to life also has Western equivalents, and other motifs—the painter's poverty or drunkenness—are stock anecdotes discussed by Kris and Kurz, including some from Japan, attributed to Hokusai.[102]

[97] Postscript, Yourcenar (1990: 145). On the popularity of Chinese stories at the time, from Malraux to Pearl Buck and Hergé, see Lescart 21.

[98] See Allamand 12 on prefaces that obstruct access to text. A majority of critics have taken Yourcenar's assertion about the Daoist fable at face value: Laude 83; Vásquez de Parga 100; Julien 120; Zhu 1282; Grassi 75, and Song 85. Conversely, only a few have taken a critical distance toward Yourcenar's assertion, recognizing the source as (pseudo-) Japanese.

[99] Hearn 1901: 37–54. Hearn's Orientalist retelling of his sparser source-text, fellow novelist Kôsai Ishikawa's *Yasô Kidan* (published in translation as *Ghost stories for the Night Lecture* in 1894), included embellishments that found their way into Yourcenar's tale, such as the noise made by the oars of the approaching boat: Inaga 117–120. Inaga's finding is referenced in Hayashi 247, Zhang 316, and Lescart 22.

[100] On the rewriting of the Ma Liang legend, see Zhang 316–320, Lescart 22 and Song 85–92.

[101] The last one was included for its artist theme, despite not being Oriental (Yourcenar 147). Painters and painting feature prominently in other Yourcenar stories from the Thirties: Terneuil 54.

[102] Kris and Kurz 47, 95, 127–128. The Japanese translator of Kris and Kurz's book, Hiroshi Oonishi, compiled Japanese artist anecdotes in an appendix to his translation, published in 1989: Inaga 120.

"How Wang-Fo Was Saved" is also a late Orientalist variation on the Romantic myth of the artist, which often reworked the earlier legendary material into tragic versions, combining the rejection of mimesis with the art-vs-life drama. The story's two cross-dressing episodes (Ling posed as a princess while his wife posed as an archer) combine the Daoist idea that art shows the essence of things rather than their appearance,[103] with the Romantic idea that art eschews imitation: "No woman was sufficiently unreal to be his model, but Ling would do because he was not a woman... No young man of the present was sufficiently unreal to serve as his model, but Ling got his own wife to pose under the plum tree in the garden" (5–6). Dressed up in Oriental garb, we recognize the theory expounded by the foundational artist narrative of modernity, Balzac's *Unknown Masterpiece*. "It's not the mission of art to copy nature, but to express it! Remember, artists aren't mere imitators, they're poets!" the painter Frenhofer exclaims.[104] Along with this grand ambition comes renunciation to life and love, and the sacrifice of model to image—the basic plot of Romantic artist novels. Wang-Fo, the Emperor knows, has no time for women, like other Romantic artist heroes who channel their erotic energy into their painting: "the silken scroll is the only mistress you ever deigned to touch" (16). Despite her beauty and devotion to her husband, Ling's wife is no match for the lure of painting. "As Ling came to prefer the portraits painted by Wang-Fo to the young woman herself" (6), she soon dies, and is promptly absorbed into her image: "Wang-Fo painted her one last time, because he loved the green hue that suffused the face of the dead. His disciple Ling mixed the colors and the task needed such concentration that he forgot to shed tears" (6). Here Romantic intertexts loom large: as Inaga facetiously points out, Yourcenar's death omens that sadden the young wife are superfluous to any reader familiar with Poe's "Oval Portrait".[105]

"Wang-Fo" is also a painterly variant on the king-and-ascetic dialogue, with the key motifs of the story redistributed in unexpected ways. Growing up in complete seclusion in the palace, the emperor only knew the world through Wang-Fo's scrolls (12–13). The shock of leaving the

---

[103] Laude 84.

[104] Balzac (2001: 13).

[105] Inaga 122. On the sacrificial structure of the romantic artist story and the rivalry between creation and procreation, see also Jullien (1992: 293–296).

palace and encountering a reality different from its painted version was as traumatic for him as it was for Siddharta, but the disappointment was aesthetic rather than existential: "At sixteen I saw the doors that separated me from the world open once again; I climbed onto the balcony of my palace to look at the clouds, but they were far less beautiful than those in your sunsets" (13). Contempt for his own empire ("The only empire which is worth reigning over is that which you alone can enter, old Wang", 13) is followed by a perverted renunciation. Filled "with disgust at everything [he] own[s], and with desire for everything [he] shall never possess" (14), the emperor resolves to blind Wang-Fo and cut off his hands, and orders Ling beheaded when he tries to defend his master (14). In Yourcenar's dark reversal of the Buddha legend, the emperor's encounter with the ascetic artist leads not to enlightenment, but bitterness, anger, and an untamed ego.[106]

If the emperor is a failed Buddha, other characters follow the righteous path of enlightenment. The story opens with a description of painter and disciple as poor ascetics "wandering along the roads of the kingdom of Han" (3). Ling's renunciation of worldly ties is another prerequisite: "One after the other, Ling sold his slaves, his jades, and the fish in his pond to buy his master pots of purple ink that came from the West. When the house was emptied, they left it, and Ling closed the door of his past behind him" (6). In this sense, "Wang-Fo" is a story about enlightenment within a story about art.[107] Ling's initiation is to wisdom rather than art: he is content to serve his master and mix his colors,[108] and of course he provides the means of escaping the emperor's cruel sentence at the end of the story. Ling's supernatural return, wearing "a strange red scarf" around his neck (18), come to spirit his master away into the picture, opens up a space of fantastic undecidability: is the tale a Taoist apologue about renouncing the ego? Is it a traditional Chinese ghost story? An artist anecdote about art's magical powers? An allegory of the impersonality of art?[109] Or is it a narrative reawakening of

---

[106] Zhu 1282.

[107] Chinese painting is conceived in quasi-mystical terms, as the revelation of secrets (Cheng 226; quoted in Julien 124).

[108] Zhu 1282.

[109] Filaire 66.

the topos of the boat of life, gliding down the water of time to disappear into the sunset of death, thereby suggesting a darker meaning for the old painter's cry "Let us leave" (19)?[110] In Borges's later "Parable of the Palace", the Yellow Emperor's wrath against the Poet who robbed him of his palace leaves readers with a mystery unresolved: so, too, does the final vanishing act of "How Wang-Fo Was Saved", Yourcenar's short and enigmatic Oriental tale.

7   POETRY AS RENUNCIATION: YI MUN-YOL'S *THE POET*

> He left then, and more than twenty years passed before he met the Old Drunkard again; but from that moment he had within him a strong inkling that there was a possibility for life to be full of poetry as such, and a notion that the true poet is one who has renounced everything.[111]

Considering they were published in the dark years of rising totalitarianism, Yourcenar's *Oriental Tales* may appear removed from politics. "Wang-Fo"'s exotic, fairy tale atmosphere, its magical solution to the political threat, could be criticized for proposing a blithely disengaged view of the world.[112] Indeed, Yourcenar in those years was not (yet) deeply political.[113] Nevertheless, the story can also be read as an allusion to totalitarianism, since it sets up a dichotomy between the peaceful empire of art ("the only empire worth reigning over", as the envious emperor acknowledges) and the very real violence unleashed on his people by a mad ruler. The book's publication coincided with Hitler's book-burning episodes (in particular May 10, 1933, in Berlin), a prelude to greater crimes.[114] Each of our four renunciation stories cross-read in

---

[110]Filaire (61–63) reads the ending as a euphemistic death narrative. Naturally the children's version, which also leaves out Ling's sacrificial wife, is more like a fairy tale, with illustrations evoking the playful magic of *Harold and the Purple Crayon*.

[111]Mun-yol 123.

[112]Howard 81.

[113]Only later, in her American career, would she take active positions on Civil Rights, the Vietnam War and environmental causes: Barbier 9–10.

[114]Lescart 28.

the Borgesian web fictionalizes a complex and ambivalent engagement with power. The fourth, Yi Mun-yol's *The Poet* (originally published in 1991), is the most overtly political, and was in fact read as a political allegory in Korea. A novel of artistic renunciation set in nineteenth-century Korea, it weaves the art theme into a greater picture of political injustice.

The Poet is a fictionalized biography of the famous Kim Pyong-yon (1807–1863). Affectionately nicknamed Kim Sakkat or "Bamboo Hat Kim", for the large hat he wore in all seasons, the wandering beggar poet came from a prominent but politically disgraced family. During the Great Insurrection of 1811–1812, the hero's grandfather was captured by rebel forces and collaborated with them, then was executed as a traitor when government forces defeated the rebels. By law, a traitor's family was also guilty: the estate was confiscated and the entire family sentenced to death. To save his sons, then aged four and six, their father sent them away with one of the family's serfs, to be raised as his own sons. Although the death sentence was eventually lifted, the burden of guilt would always remain. After the father died of consumption, mother and children wandered destitute from one village to the next, ostracized as traitor's kin. The future poet grew up profoundly embittered by social and political injustice. After years spent vainly trying to regain his place in society, he left everything behind and donning his proverbial bamboo hat set off on the road. Kim's achievement as a poet is inseparable from his self-imposed withdrawal from society.

The story of Kim's poetic itinerary is woven into Korea's violent history.[115] Furthermore, *The Poet* also resonates with the author's personal history. Yi Mun-yol's father, a Communist sympathizer, defected to North Korea in 1951, exposing his family to years of discrimination.[116] Like his nineteenth-century hero, Yi Mun-yol had "to live under a burden of a sin he did not commit yet [could] not deny".[117] The analogy,

[115] On the intertwining of modern Korean literature and its sociopolitical context, see Fulton 628.

[116] The Author's preface acknowledged the similarities as a motivation: Mun-yol xiv. The belated encounter between Yi Mun-yol and his North Korean half-brother is the subject of the memoir *An Appointment with my Brother* (1994).

[117] On this sin and its resemblance to the original sin of Catholicism, a religion introduced into Korean culture via the Jesuit missionaries in China, see Mun-yol ix.

immediately familiar to Korean readers, prompted an allegorical reading of the novel filtered through contemporary history, especially the Cold War partition of Korea.[118]

The successive phases of Kim Sakkat's poetic career follow his unsuccessful attempts to make a place for himself in society. Ostracism proves insurmountable. In nineteenth-century Korea, access to lucrative positions in the imperial bureaucracy required knowledge of the Chinese classics and skill at composing poetry in the intricate formal style.[119] When Kim wins first prize at a local poetry contest, the distinction should in principle pave the way for a government post, allowing him to restore the family's status. But Kim finds himself in a cruel double bind between duty to his family and loyalty to the state. The poetry contest's topic called for praising the general who died fighting the rebels and denouncing the one who surrendered to them—his own grandfather. Having poured his pent-up anger into a poem that excoriates the traitor, Kim then feels too guilty to collect his prize, and instead drowns his shame in a tavern where a stranger reviles him mercilessly: "The grandfather sold the king to buy his own wretched life; now here's the grandson busy selling his own grandfather to buy himself honours" (70).[120] Far from gaining social recognition from his poetic skill, he must flee in disgrace when his identity becomes known (74–75). The traumatic pattern repeats itself when he goes to Seoul to attempt the state examination, a process so corrupt that only the sons of upper-class families are considered while others cannot even secure a place in the room (86). Abandoning the hope of promotion through examination, he attaches himself to a wealthy family as a

---

[118] All the more since Mun-yol's earlier novel, *Our Twisted Hero*, a semi-autobiographical story about the rise and fall of a small-town bully, was meant to be understood as an allegory of Korea's political history: Suh 727. On Yi Mun-yol's pessimistic view of society, see Riotto 534–535.

[119] In premodern times poetry was the measure of an educated man, professionally and personally. It conferred tangible class benefits. A mastery of poetry, acquired through years of arduous schooling, was essential for government office and hence was tested in the civil service exam that granted admission to the ranks of the scholar-bureaucrat literati who administered the nation. The composition of poetry was an omnipresent recreational activity among men, with public displays of virtuosity and impromptu challenges (Fulton 625; 630).

[120] This stranger turns out to be Noh Jin, another political outcast. See note 124. Noh Jin returns a second time, twenty years later, to condemn the Poet's "popular" poetry, which expresses support for his grandfather's actions, thus aggravating the double bind that ensnares Kim.

guest poet under a pseudonym, only to be unmasked and cast out once more (99). The humiliation he suffers as his political and social ambitions are crushed, his dreams for life in society curtailed, his chances of personal happiness thwarted, has no redeeming transcendence, unlike tragedy in the Western sense of the word: instead it tells a story of what Korean literature calls *han*, a bitterness that turns the hero inward in self-destruction.[121]

The Poet can also be read as the reverse image of a Western *Bildungsroman*, since, far from securing a place in society in the end, the hero opts instead for self-imposed exclusion.[122] Only when he renounces all attachments, abandoning his family and unmooring himself from any place or position, does the Poet begin to realize his vocation. The novel ends when the Poet's son, come to take him home, decides instead to let him go, realizing that confining him to domesticity would annihilate him as a poet (196–197).[123]

Among the many substitute father figures in the novel, an especially intriguing one is the Old Drunkard, who crosses paths with the Poet at two pivotal moments. Despite his low social status as a drifter and a drunk, he radiates an aura of wisdom and authority. The insight gained from him helps Kim spread his wings as a poet, while at the same time tearing his poetic vocation away from any social ambition. It thereby confirms the bitter lesson taught by another outcast, the scholar Noh Jin: in the face of corruption, the only path is renunciation.[124]

The first meeting with the Old Drunkard, in the dead center of the book, leads the Poet to abandon his wife and young children: like the Buddha, he walks away in the night while they sleep (124–125).

---

[121] On *han* as the Korean counterpart to Western tragedy, see the translators' introduction, x–xi.

[122] Koh 644–645.

[123] This double renunciation echoes the earlier semi-autobiographical trilogy, *A Portrait of my Youth* (1981), which chronicles an adolescent's identity search outside the family structure: Koh 646.

[124] Confucius's *Analects* advise that when the emperor is unjust, the just man should desist: "A great minister serves his ruler by means of the Way, and if he can't, he will quit" (Confucius 11:22). Noh Jin is another victim of the unjust political system: because he comes from the historically rebellious northwestern region, he is not even allowed to compete in the public examinations, and makes a miserable living as a wandering teacher (66). On Noh Jin's scathing criticism of Kim, see Note 120.

After the second meeting twenty years later the Poet surrenders any hope of social integration and begins his final enlightenment (188). If the novel is a reverse *Bildungsroman*, perhaps the Old Drunkard is a reverse father figure, symbolizing the severance of all social and familial ties that weigh so heavily upon the Confucian world, and the liberation from the family "sin" that has consumed the hero and others around him.[125] Combining wisdom and squalor, espousing marginality in order to critique society's ills, the Old Drunkard also seems a Korean counterpart to a Greek Cynic. In dialogue with him the hero renounces palatial ambition for the pared-down life of the wandering ascetic. "It's only when all [social ties have] been thrown overboard that the true poet is born", the Old Drunkard pronounces (116), defining poetry as "mind and body casting off their bonds" (119). The blood that the Poet coughs up after each life-changing encounter serves ambiguously to align him with his father (who died of consumption) but also, conversely, to distance himself from his unliberated father: by spitting out the blood ties that bind he breaks free from the stifling web of obligations.[126] The father-son bond is finally severed when Kim Sakkat's son renounces him: "The man moving away in the glimmering darkness was not his father. He was a poet, and nothing else" (198).

This contemporary variation on the Asian tradition of scholar-as-renouncer[127] intersects the Western artist novel, as we follow Kim Sakkat's itinerary as a poet and an outcast under "the star of deviation that was guiding his life" (166). The process first requires him to renounce the highly rhetorical official poetic style he has mastered. His next phases are as a satirical "people's poet", mocking the aristocracy for the entertainment of the lower classes (Chapter 27), then a revolutionary poet, able to whip up rebellion with his poems (Chapter 32). But his last period is mystical. As he withdraws ever further from world, language, and self, he is refined into near-invisibility (192–193). Going beyond skill, his poetry

---

[125] That this liberation is in no way guilt-free is symbolized by the bamboo hat, which serves to shield the Poet from the weather but also from his guilt at abandoning his family (104–105).

[126] This occurs after the poetry contest (70), when he leaves his family (125), when he finally cuts emotional ties to his grandfather (162). See Fulton 628 on the omnipresent theme of confinement, whether physical, spiritual, political, or psychological, in Korean literature.

[127] On scholar-renouncers in the Chinese cultural context, and on the topical emperor-renouncer relations, see Yongjia 7–15.

ends up going beyond words. Just as the Old Drunkard was called a poet, not on the basis of actual compositions, but because of his ability to commune with nature (122), so in the end, Kim Sakkat vanishes into the landscape because, in Buddhist or Taoist fashion, he has reached "a concept of poetry that has nothing at all to do with words, techniques or themes, but with being".[128] One of his poems captures this: "Changed to a crane, the hermit flies off, no knowing where" (129). Kim Sakkat disappears—into his poem, into nature, into death—like Yourcenar's Wang-Fo who vanished into his own painting, and Borges's poet in "The Mirror and the Mask", who transcended poetic skill to such a degree that both poet and listener were obliterated by a single ineffable poem.[129]

8   THE MYSTERY OF RENUNCIATION

In the end, art itself is swept up in the renunciatory process. Kim Sakkat's poetic trajectory resonates with the lives of artists, philosophers, and writers compiled by Ross Posnock, whose inquiry on renunciation as a creative principle climaxes with the "painterly undoing" of Agnes Martin.[130] Taking detachment from fame and fortune as far as Kim Sakkat, Martin (who was profoundly influenced by Asian philosophy)[131] sought a comparably radical "divestment from self".[132]

The artist characters examined here share this mystical conception of creation, which isolates the artistic experience as ineffable, incommunicable, and severed from both medium and audience.[133] Sacrificing everything to his maligned labyrinth, Ts'ui Pen, the hidden hero of "The Garden of Forking Paths", accepts his descendants' misunderstanding

---

[128] Translators' introduction, xi.

[129] Like Kim Sakkat, Borges's poet refined his art from a perfectly crafted product in the rhetorical tradition of the *kenningar* to the "startling opacity" of a magic spell: Heller-Roazen 43.

[130] Posnock 375. Martin (1912–2004) left the circle of Abstract Impressionists in New York City as her career was taking off, renouncing painting for seven years to become a hermit in New Mexico. Only then did she start painting again, in her signature ascetic style that is rather a kind of painterly meditation.

[131] Martin, who attended Suzuki's seminar in the early Fifties, practiced daily meditation, and retained a lifelong interest in Buddhism, Taoism and Christian mysticism (Posnock 367).

[132] Posnock 367.

[133] Posnock 78.

and contempt. No one before Stephen Albert understood his project, except, tellingly, "a Taoist or Buddhist monk": the masterpiece's invisibility behind the "contradictory jumble of irresolute drafts" is an essential part of the renunciatory scheme (*CF* 124). A key requirement of the creative process in many of Borges's poet stories is renunciation, taken to self-annihilating extremes as the act itself is refined into invisibility, delivering the ascetic to public scorn.

In "The Rose of Paracelsus", one of the last Borges stories, the alchemist refuses to perform magic for the traveling student, thereby renouncing his reputation. After the student leaves, concealing his disappointment and contemptuous pity under the forms of deference, Paracelsus "poured the delicate fistful of ashes from one hand to the concave other, and he whispered a single word. The rose appeared again" (*CF* 507). His ascetic estrangement from his audience exemplifies what Susan Sontag termed the "priestly" aims of avant-garde art, one that reveals itself only to initiates.[134] This "aesthetics of silence"[135] also commands the student's withholding the results of his research in "The Ethnographer". After two years spent studying the secret rites of a Native American tribe for a dissertation that could lead to a successful academic career, Fred Murdock's decision not to publish combines the initiate's secrecy with the avant-garde artist's refusal to verbalize his mystical experience. "I learned something out there that I can't express", he tells his professor (*CF* 135). Beyond its obvious ethical or political motives (the refusal to profit from the tribe's secret or condone Western imperialist knowledge),[136] Murdock's renunciatory gesture also follows a recognizably aesthetic precedent, making him an honorary member of Posnock's renunciant artists' society. These renunciation stories eschew intelligibility, *preferring not to* justify the baffling and apparently self-destructive gesture at their heart. Fred will no more explain his withdrawal to his professor than Borges explains it to the reader. Fred's epitome of a non-life provides the terse ending of the story: "Fred married, divorced, and is now one of the librarians at Yale" (335). The opacity of these

---

[134] Sontag 295–296; quoted in Posnock 134.

[135] Posnock 135, applied to Duchamp and Rimbaud. Also see Posnock reading Blanchot reading Rimbaud, linking Rimbaud's renunciation to the mystical goal he ascribed to poetry (18).

[136] Both reasons are argued by Nichanian 7–8.

stories brings to mind the "candid nihilism" (*SNF* 246)[137] of Bartleby the Scrivener, "American literature's iconic renunciant".[138]

8.1   Charms O'erthrown: *Prospero's Shadow*

A fork in the path of poetic renunciation leads to Shakespeare, whose abrupt surrender fueled Borges's imagination. Prospero's decision to drown his book and renounce his magic at the end of *The Tempest* is traditionally interpreted as an allusion to Shakespeare's own retirement from the theater, an act of abandonment both final and unexplained. Prospero's shadow hangs over Borges's final collection, *Shakespeare's Memory*, whose four stories are intricate variations on the renunciation motif.[139] Borges's ambiguous farewell story, "Shakespeare's Memory",[140] returns to the mystery surrounding Shakespeare's life and final silence. A German scholar, Hermann Sörgel, receives from a stranger the memory of Shakespeare—a cursed gift thanks to which he presumes, naïvely, that he will be able to write the definitive biography about the famously unknown man behind the author. Time passes and strange memories begin to bubble up to his consciousness (*CF* 512). Eventually, he is no longer able to distinguish Shakespeare's memories from Sörgel's; Shakespeare's "great torrent", welcome at first, threatens "to flood [his] own modest stream" (514). More bitterly, he also comes to realize that the individual's memories will not help him penetrate the playwright's genius: "Chance, or fate, dealt Shakespeare those trivial terrible things that all men know; it was his gift to be able to transmute them into fables, into characters that were much more alive than the gray man who dreamed them, into verses which will never be abandoned, into verbal music. What purpose would it serve to unravel that

---

[137] Borges also notes the retrospective affinity of "Bartleby the Scrivener" with Kafka's tales: "Kafka's work casts a curious ulterior light on 'Bartleby'" (ibid.).

[138] Posnock 175.

[139] "25 August 1983" stages a dialogue between a younger, more ambitious "Borges" and an older, sadder "Borges" who has committed suicide, renouncing his unfinished book and his life. "Blue Tigers" is analyzed in Chapter 4.

[140] Although "Shakespeare's Memory" was not the last story published (it appeared in 1980), Borges later decided to put the story in final place, using its title for the entire volume, clearly giving it prominence and closure. On the compositional history of the final collection, see *OCP* II: 1444–1446.

wondrous fabric, besiege and mine the tower, reduce to the modest proportions of a documentary biography or a realistic novel the sound and
fury of *Macbeth?*" (514). The finest biography in the world will never
be written.[141] Weary, disillusioned, fearing for his sanity, the narrator
decides that he wants "to be Hermann Sörgel again" (514) and gets rid
of Shakespeare's memory by giving it to another man. He renounces the
possibility of being a world or an "ocean" (510),[142] to be "simply the
thing [he is]" (515)—nothing more than "Professor Emeritus Hermann
Sörgel", composer of "erudite trivialities" (515).

Cross-read with two other texts about Shakespeare, the 1950 essay
"From Someone to Nobody" and the parable "*Everything and Nothing*",
the negative epiphany experienced by Sörgel recasts the renunciation trope
derived from Buddhism in the light of Shakespeare's own legendary renunciation to the theater. "From Someone to Nobody" reflects on the ways
in which monotheistic theology has attempted to express the idea of an
all-encompassing divinity. In an unexpected shift, the second half of the
essay is devoted to Shakespeare, whom the Romantics worshipped as a god:
"A magnification to nothingness occurs or tends to occur in all cults; we
may observe it unmistakably in the case of Shakespeare". For Coleridge,
Shakespeare was "no longer a man but a literary variation of the infinite
God of Spinoza"; for Hazlitt "he was nothing in himself", which enabled
him to be all men; Hugo "compared him to the ocean, which is the seed-
bed of all possible forms" (342).[143] Shakespeare's reception history intersects with the metaphysical speculations on individuality which inform
so many of Borges's essays: "To be something is inexorably not to be all
the other things; the confused intuition of this truth has induced mankind to imagine that being nothing is more than being something and
is, in some way, to be everything" (342). The equation of nothing with
everything comes full circle by tying Shakespeare's legend to the Buddha's,
"that legendary king of India who renounces power and goes out to beg
in the streets", claiming "From this day forward I have no realm or my

---

[141] Unsurprisingly, perhaps, Borges's deathbed story pays homage to his favorite Kipling
story, "The Finest Story in the World".

[142] This alludes to Victor Hugo, who called Shakespeare "un homme-océan" at the
beginning of *William Shakespeare* (12, 159). On Borges's reworking of Hugo's genius
myth, see Jullien (1995: 145–152).

[143] The poem "Herman Melville" connects the ocean metaphor with the idea of literary
archetypes: "that other ocean, which is Writing, and... the outline of the archetypes" (*SP* 377).

realm is limitless" (343). It provides a metaphysical subtext to the melancholy Sörgel's experience of renouncing Shakespeare's infinite memory and resigning himself to being, unfortunately, Sörgel.[144]

The parable titled, in English, *"Everything and Nothing"*[145] builds on the myth that Romantics have elaborated on the biographical void surrounding Shakespeare.[146] Borges takes this void as his point of departure, turning the lack of data into an existential condition. "There was no one inside him", the story begins (*CF* 318). Shakespeare turned to the stage in order to conceal his "nobodiness" (319) behind the multiplicity of roles; but one day, feeling overwhelmed, like Sörgel, by the hallucinatory identities, he sold his theater, returned to Stratford, and since "he had to be somebody" (320), assumed his last role, that of a retired businessman, in which capacity he penned his notorious will, one of the few documents that bear witness to his individual existence. Borges's parable ends with a dialogue in heaven between Shakespeare and God, where the Romantic trope of Shakespeare-as-God is spun out literally: "God's voice answered him out of a whirlwind: *I, too, am not I; I dreamed the world as you, Shakespeare, dreamed your own work, and among the forms of my dream are you, who like me are many, yet no one*" (320).

Twenty years later, as Borges was nearing the end of his life, "Shakespeare's Memory" revisited the themes of *"Everything and Nothing"*, but in a sadder, more resigned mode; renunciation to art—whether the ocean of forms that made up Shakespeare's Globe, or the more modest biography that was to be Hermann Sörgel's *magnum opus*—was the end toward which the stories pointed. Migrating from the religious and political spheres into the core of the creative process, renunciation aligned the ascetic with the artist: whether life was sacrificed to art, or—more mysteriously—renunciation to art was itself the *telos*. These narratives exemplify the "estrangement from the immediately intelligible that marks aesthetic experience",[147] hinting at a transcendence that defeats normal meaning-making. The kinship of renunciation stories with the enigmatic genre of modern parables, which also elude understanding, is the topic of Chapter 4.

---

[144]Compare the conclusion to the famous essay "A New Refutation of Time": "The world, unfortunately, is real; I, unfortunately, am Borges" (*SNF* 332).

[145]The two texts were positioned side by side in *PA* (115, 118).

[146]See Novillo-Corvalán 2008 on the interface between Borges's Shakespeare parables, Joyce's *Ulysses*, and Romantic myths of Shakespeare, in particular Coleridge.

[147]Posnock 16.

CHAPTER 4

Modernity's Enigmatic Parables of Renunciation

Abstract This chapter frames the renunciation stories within the broader question of modern parables, which appeal to and yet also frustrate readers' longing for certain meaning, exemplarity, or revelation. In a post-transcendent context, the story's straightforward efficiency is lost, along with its spiritual or political agency. This chapter engages with the enigmatic nature of the parable-like variants on the Renunciation story, both in Borges and beyond, in parables by Kafka and Blixen.

Keywords Parable · Kafka · Blixen · Revelation · Enigma · Benjamin

> ... because the machine of the world is exceedingly complex for the simplicity of a savage beast.[1]

1   Borgesian Parables and the Enigmatic Mode

"My stories are not meant to be parables"; "my intention has never been to write parables".[2] Borges's surprising denial of the parabolic nature of his writing, reiterated in interviews and prologues, deserves clarification. He appears to make no difference between moral stories, allegories, parables, fables or modern-day engaged novels. The Foreword to *Brodie's*

---

[1] *"Inferno* I, 32", *CF* 323.
[2] Christ 266.

© The Author(s) 2019
D. Jullien, *Borges, Buddhism and World Literature*, Literatures of the Americas, https://doi.org/10.1007/978-3-030-04717-7_4

Report elaborates in greater detail: "I am not what used to be called a fabulist or a spinner of parables, what these days is called an *auteur engagé*. I do not aspire to be Aesop. My tales, like those of the *1001 Nights*, are intended not to persuade readers, but to entertain and touch them".[3]

What Borges rejects, then, is the use of narrative as a vehicle for an explicit moral, political or ideological message,[4] what Susan Rubin Suleiman termed "authoritarian fictions".[5] But while they lack the rhetorical strategy and pragmatic goal associated with fables, exempla or ideological fictions, Borges's stories clearly conform to the very broad definition of "parable" given by the OED: "any saying or narration in which something is expressed in terms of something else".[6] More importantly, Borges is widely seen as a parable writer in the tradition of Kafka: one whose tales, whether or not their titles identify them as "parables", are short, enigmatic, and perplexing.[7] This chapter frames renunciation stories within the broader question of modern parables, which appeal to and yet also frustrate readers' longing for exemplarity or revelation. Indeed the resurgence of parables as a contemporary literary form[8] is bound up with a double and contradictory movement toward and away from interpretation. My analysis now seeks to engage with the enigmatic nature of the parable-like variants on the Renunciation story, both in Borges and beyond, in writers such as Franz Kafka and Karen Blixen.

---

[3] Foreword to *Brodie's Report*, *CF* 345.

[4] The essay on Hawthorne corroborates this position, lamenting the fact that the tales' imaginative strangeness is often spoiled by a heavy-handed moral conclusion dictated by Hawthorne's Puritanical background: *OC* 2: 48–63 (especially 49–51).

[5] "Stories with a clear ideological message (…) that seek, through the vehicle of fiction, to persuade their readers of the 'correctness' of a particular way of interpreting the world" (Suleiman 1). Her first chapter offers a structuralist analysis of parables and fables as "exemplary narratives" (25–54).

[6] Quoted by MacNiece 2.

[7] On the history of Borges's discovery of Kafka, see C. García 33–43 and Roger 142–146.

[8] Schwartz (xxi) discusses the frequency of parables in contemporary writing and advocates recognizing parables as an independent literary form.

2   PARABLES AND PARADOXES: KAFKA, BORGES AND THE MODERN DEBATE ON PARABLES

Contemporary parables, it is often argued, aim at perplexing rather than instructing. The Borgesian parables of dispossession illuminate the contemporary debate on parables and their ambiguous relation to the literature of wisdom and revelation. A nexus of contemporary criticism brings together biblical parables from the Gospels, Kafka, and Borges. A key factor in the resurgence of critical interest in parables is the centrality of Kafka's parables. Modern parables, critics claim, are ambiguous, whether in contrast to ancient parables which are deemed to be straightforward, or in the wake of the ancient parable tradition. The difference usually hinges on Kafka's place in the equation.

Heinz Politzer's seminal study, *Franz Kafka: Parable and Paradox*, saw contemporary parables as a response to the loss of spiritual certainties. In a world "depleted of metaphysical truths",[9] parables retained the search for a transcendence that remained elusive. Kafka, Politzer argued, drew on the parabolic form familiar to the religious tradition of Jewish Haggadah, but he did so, paradoxically, in order to "express his own religious uncertainties and metaphysical longings" (84). Kafka's parables convey "a profound longing for the transcendental world and an equally profound disappointment at what he found here in its stead". This disconnect between transcendental yearning and loss of faith gives them their characteristic shape. The modern parable "no longer carries a clear-cut message but is built around a paradox" (85). As modernity untethered the European Jewry from its ancestral beliefs, in Kafka's parables the word and the practice of sin remained central, but no longer meaningful.[10] This sense of meaninglessness and God-forsakenness dovetails with Walter Benjamin's diagnostic of a "sickness of tradition". Severed from the traditional truths, Kafka's parables "do not modestly lie at the feet of the doctrine, as the Haggadah lies at the feet of the Halakah. Though apparently reduced to submission, they unexpectedly raise a mighty paw against it. This is why, in regard to Kafka, we can no longer speak of wisdom. Only the products of its decay remain".[11]

---

[9] Politzer 85.

[10] McNiece 140.

[11] Benjamin 143–144. On the spiritual affinities between Benjamin and Kafka, see Alter 57–61.

Building on Politzer's analysis, Gila Safran Naveh focuses on the challenges to interpretation that parables, from their Biblical origins to modern recreations, pose to literary critics. She draws a sharp line separating early parables, clear and concise narratives with a pedagogical purpose, structurally related to fables (23), from Kafka's and Borges's impenetrable, dream-like parables (27). "Modern man's massive estrangement from his hermeneutic community and from tradition" (124), seeking in vain for a lost truth, is troped in Kafka's famous self-reflective parable "Couriers", where kings have all died and only messengers are left, shouting meaningless messages to one another. Kafka's parables, she argues, are indebted to ancient parables, yet also part ways with them: like them they allow for various interpretations, but unlike them, they are open and indeterminate rather than didactic. They also are not intended for a privileged community of insiders; rather, "to Kafka's parables we are all outsiders" (137).

Kafka is a key reference for modern parabolists—Borges, of course, but also Italo Calvino and S. Y. Agnon, among others, all claim him as precursor.[12] Yet Kafka's place in the contemporary interpretation of ancient parables is more remarkable still. So central, in fact, is Kafka to the critical debate on parables that Kafka's shadow—and often, Borges's too—extends retrospectively over ancient parables: one of the most influential parable critics builds on the Borges-inspired thesis that Jesus is a precursor of Kafka.[13]

Both Jesus and Kafka, Funk argues, were displaced Jews out of step with their traditions. Their parables are irreducible to moral exemplarity. Read through Kafka's enigmatic parables, Gospel parables are not straightforward at all, despite their apparent realism: they are akin to riddles or picture puzzles,[14] while the "kingdom of God", the subject of most Gospel parables, is aligned with the "fabulous yonder" of Kafka's parable "On Parables".[15] Contrary to common assumption, parables

---

[12] Naveh includes these heirs of Kafka alongside her discussions of Biblical parables (123–124).

[13] Robert W. Funk's *Jesus as Precursor* (1975), marked by the discovery of Kafka, according to Bernard B. Scott the crowning achievement of Funk's work on parables: Funk (2006: 1). In Funk's essay "Crossing over", Jesus, Kafka and Borges are clustered as "great tellers of parables in the West" (Funk 2006: 57–58).

[14] "The Parable as Metaphor", Funk (2006: 38).

[15] Kafka, "On Parables", p. 457. Funk (2006: 54).

about the kingdom of God offer no didactic example, no set of moral guidelines, but a much more disquieting distortion of reality; they mean to shock listeners out of their comfort zone. Such "parables of grace"[16] frustrate the audience's expectations and challenge interpretation. Paradox is their beating heart: the prodigal son is welcomed back instead of punished, the vineyard laborers are paid more if they work less, the Samaritan helps the Jew, and so forth. Jesus's parables "are not meant to be interpreted but to interpret"[17]: they are provocative, "an invitation to pass through the looking-glass".[18]

Funk's reading of Gospel parables in Kafka's retrospective light is shared, and in some sense amplified, by J. D. Crossan, who adds a layer of Borgesian intertextuality and mysticism. *The Dark Interval: Toward a Theology of Story* brings together Funk's views on Jesus as precursor of Kafka, and Ben Belitt's seminal analysis of Kafka and Borges's parables as "enigmatic predicaments".[19] Jesus, Kafka, and Borges are for him "parablers", not moralists or allegorists (99). Occupying opposite ends of the narrative spectrum, myths confidently create worlds, while parables undermine this confidence and "shatter the deep structure of our accepted world" (100). The original message of Jesus's parables has been "domesticated" by church tradition, notably by the Church Fathers, who smoothed out their rough angles and "moved them back into literary types well known from the carefully constructed pedagogical methods of the rabbis" (101),[20] for the unproblematic moral instruction of the masses. Thus the parable of the Good Samaritan was domesticated into a didactic story about neighborliness, when in fact the despised Samaritan character was initially chosen for shock value.[21]

---

[16] "Parable, Paradox and Power: The Prodigal Samaritan", Funk (2006: 134).

[17] Funk (2006: 6) (quoting Ernst Fuchs).

[18] "The Looking-glass tree is for the birds: the cedars of Lebanon", Funk (2006: 120).

[19] Crossan (1988) and Belitt 269.

[20] Crossan (1988: 100), see also Funk's introduction, pp. xi–xiii.

[21] In order to make this shock value clear, Crossan (1988: 86–87) modernizes the encounter between the Jew and the Samaritan by substituting a wounded Irish Catholic and a Protestant terrorist, or a wounded American soldier and a Viet Cong guerrilla.

Here Crossan aligns with Funk, and parts ways with Politzer.[22] The original parables, Crossan claims, were never meant as straightforward example stories: "Examples persuade but parables provoke".[23] They aim to "remove our defenses and make us vulnerable to God. It is only in such experiences that God can touch us, and only in such moments does the kingdom of God arrive".[24] This mystical interpretation of the "kingdom of God" trope retains all the enigmatic quality of Kafka's "fabulous yonder": but in addition, it also opens the human mind to a state of "transcendence" (100) germane to the post-rational experience sought by Zen Buddhism. The pursuit of "transcendence" here comes full circle: by mounting a "raid on the articulate", moving beyond the aporetical unease where Kafka's parables leave us, these disruptive stories point to a Borgesian epiphany, imminent yet unrealized, and they bring Jesus's message in resonance with the non-verbal experience of *satori*.

Critics reading the Gospel parables as precursors, in the Borgesian sense, of Kafka (and in some cases also of Borges) understand parables as inherently destabilizing, "meta-didactic stories"[25] built around an irreducible core of enigma. Their Jesus has read Kafka, and often Borges as well. In the wake of Structuralist criticism of the Gospels,[26] their approach turns away from traditional practices of *exegesis* in favor of secular literary *reading*, treating parables as aesthetic objects, as fictions not formally distinct from Kafka's or Borges's.[27] As Jesus's parables come to resemble Kafka's or Borges's, they relinquish sacred authority in exchange for a literary kind of transcendence closer to Borges's reticent epiphany.[28]

---

[22] He borrowed Politzer's title "Paradox and Parable" for the "Third Variation" of his earlier book *Raid on the Articulate:* Crossan (1976: 93).

[23] Crossan (1976: 104).

[24] Crossan (1988: 100).

[25] Politzer 352, quoted by Crossan (1976: 113).

[26] See Marin 93–192 as well as Suleiman 262–263, who relies on Structuralist readings by Starobinski, Barthes and Todorov.

[27] This is noted—and criticized—by Perrin 342–344.

[28] On the Borgesian space between "hopeful aspiration and... negative limitation or failure", see Irby 47 quoted by Crossan (1976: 114).

3 KAFKA'S IRONIC RENUNCIATION PARABLE:
"A HUNGER ARTIST"

Kafka's parables speak of lost transcendence and absent or undeliverable messages. "On Parables" metatextually sums up the predicament with a message about the absence of a message, while its mirror image, "An Imperial Message" tells of waiting for a message that can never be delivered, and "Couriers" reflects the chaos of a world in which the senders of the message have gone missing.[29] Such parables merely reveal the opacity of the world and the futility of the quest for meaning.

In Kafka's deathbed story, "A Hunger Artist", the character, who performs impossible feats of self-denial as a form of entertainment, is both an ascetic hero and an artist figure, bridging the realms of spirituality and creativity. As Breon Mitchell has shown, Kafka's unnamed hero is closely modeled on historical hunger artists whose popularity as a form of pseudo-scientific spectacle peaked before World War I, when newer, more exciting displays (especially motion pictures) relegated them to traveling freak shows.[30] Many critics read "A Hunger Artist" as a self-portrait, both because Kafka's late stories—among them "Josephine the Singer" or "First Sorrow"—tend to be portraits of the artist,[31] and because Kafka himself, whose relation to food was always complicated, was starving to death as a result of tuberculosis.[32]

Kafka's self-portrait as an ascetic artist also speaks to his admiration for Flaubert, in whose heroic self-denial he recognized his own struggles.[33] The Hunger Artist, a counterpart to Anthony and other Flaubertian artist saints, has also been interpreted as a modernist descendant of the misunderstood Romantic artist, heroically attempting to suppress normal physical functions and control the flux of time by fasting into eternity. In spite of his downward trajectory from the theater to the circus, where he lies forgotten in a cage next to the animals, his record-breaking prowess unrecorded, the Hunger Artist still believes his unappreciated art is worthy of the ultimate sacrifice: to him "the last conversation constitutes

[29] Kafka (1972: 11, 13, 175).

[30] Kafka's character especially resembles the most famous of these, the Italian Giovanni Succi: Mitchell 236–255.

[31] Thiher 80.

[32] Ogden 350–352.

[33] Degner 75.

an art-death analogous to the Wagnerian love-death".[34] If anything the public's lack of appreciation is itself a requirement of the ascetic artist's ideal, as seen in the previous chapter.

Yet, as critics have shown, the grand renunciatory narrative is thrown into disarray in the parable's final turn that exposes the hero's ascetic posturing as a fraud, depriving his self-inflicted pain of redemptive virtue. Thus, while "A Hunger Artist" belongs in the late group of artist stories, it also makes sense to pair it with earlier stories focused on law and punishment, which also problematize the idea of the redemptive benefit of pain. The Hunger Artist's deathbed confession to the Overseer ("I couldn't find the food I liked", 277) undercuts the supposed transcendence of his fasting, reducing the ascetic exploit (superhuman control of body) to a serendipitous condition (lack of appetite or zest for life). Confusing a dramatic performance with a saintly denial doomed the Hunger Artist's quest from the start in any case.[35] Both for the Hunger Artist and the Officer in "The Penal Colony", whose tortured bodies end up thrown out like garbage, the case for transcendence was spurious to begin with; Kafka's renunciant hero "exposes the fraudulent modern teleologies of suffering".[36]

4   BORGES'S RENUNCIATION PARABLES: EPIPHANY, RENOUNCED

Even in the more realistic stories of *Brodie's Report* (1970), which explicitly emulated Kipling's "plain" tales, Borges underlined the importance of retaining a kernel of mystery, and eschewing simplicity, a meaningless goal: "there is not a simple page, a simple word, on earth—for all pages, all words, predicate the universe, whose most notorious attribute is its complexity".[37] Borges's celebrated definition of the aesthetic fact as "imminence of a revelation that doesn't happen"[38] captured this crucial

---

[34] Rolleston 139–140.

[35] Melchionne 147, 143.

[36] Norris 432 reads the story in light of Nietzsche's ironic debunking of the ascetic artist mythology in *On the Genealogy of Morality*, see also Geddes who analyzes the Officer's spurious claim to moral redemption through Lévinas's discussion of "useless suffering". "The justification of the neighbor's pain is certainly the source of all immorality" (Lévinas 99, quoted in Geddes 127).

[37] Foreword to *Brodie's Report*, *CF* 345 (translation modified).

[38] "The Wall and the Books", *SNF* 346 (translation modified).

requirement of ambiguity. Looking at two stories of kingly dispossession written almost forty years apart, "The Writing of the God" from *The Aleph* (1949) and the late story "Blue Tigers" from *Shakespeare's Memory* (1983) brings to light how these variations on the king-and-ascetic pattern carry an uncertain or perplexing outcome in keeping with the frustrated search for transcendence—for the failure of teleological revelation—that characterizes contemporary parables.

4.1   Understanding the Writing on the Tiger

In "The Writing of the God", the king and the ascetic are fused: Tzinacán, priest of the Mayan pyramid of Qaholom, tortured and imprisoned by the Spanish conquistador Pedro de Alvarado, is both ascetic and king, both everything and nothing. His empire destroyed, his temple burnt, his body maimed, he has been utterly dispossessed and reduced to nothing, a dying man in a dark cell. Yet years of doggedly studying the god's secret writing have granted him potential omniscience and omnipotence: at the heart of the story, a syncretistic, Aleph-like epiphany displays the Wheel "of all the things that shall be, that are, and that have been... the causes and the effects... the universe and... its secret designs" (*CF* 253).[39] This revelation offers Tzinacán the power to change the universe, to reverse the course of history: "Speaking [the magic formula] would make this stone prison disappear, allow the day to enter my night, make me young, make me immortal, make the jaguar destroy Alvarado, bury the sacred blade in Spanish breasts, rebuild the Pyramid, rebuild the empire" (253). But the story ends on a paradoxical and devastating reversal: "Tzinacán, who deciphers the highest mystery of his religion... chooses to let it die with him".[40] Having the power to "rule the lands once ruled by Moctezuma", Tzinacán renounces it because he now is— or wants to be—nothing and no one: "I no longer remember Tzinacán". Like the Buddha, and also like the alchemist Paracelsus,[41] Tzinacán

---

[39] On the blurring of cultural boundaries in the story, which intermingles "Maya, Aztec and Quiché elements with Kabbalistic themes [and] Hindu and Buddhist ideas", see Fishburn in Williamson (2013: 58). On the parallels with the Zen experience of loss of self, see Flynn 132.

[40] Kristal (2002: xiii).

[41] "The Rose of Paracelsus", *CF* 504–507, see Chapter 3.

forgoes individuality in favor of fusion in the greater cosmic scheme: "He who has glimpsed the universe... can have no thought for a man, for a man's trivial joys or calamities, though he himself be that man" (253–254).

4.2   "No Way Out of the Chaos"

In "Blue Tigers", the ascetic and kingly roles are reshuffled. The imperially named Alexander Craigie, proud Scotsman, confident philosopher, and "professor of Eastern and Western logic" (*CF* 494) at the University of Lahore, is a scholar, like so many Borgesian heroes, but also a "king" in the manner of Kipling. His quest for an elusive blue tiger leads him to the blue stones; their discovery annihilates the logic that he stands for, causing him to renounce his sense of control and superiority. The blue stones that proliferate inexplicably in "cancer-like growth"[42] bring with them a horrifying revelation of Kafkaesque irrationality: in a universe that "can tolerate disorder" (500), there is "no way out of the chaos" (502). The story's esoteric web unravels in the ambivalent ending, which reverses the gift protocol: by giving away his cursed treasure to the blind beggar, he recovers his world (503) but abandons his unwarranted assurance.[43] The mutual gift on which this open-ended story concludes leaves us in the limbo of revelation withheld or suspended. "I did not hear the blind beggar's steps, or see him disappear into the dawn" (503). Having attained the secret, Tzinacán gives it up. Having been granted the talisman, Craigie gives it away. In both parables of renunciation, as in Blixen's "Consolatory Tale" where the story is passed on but no one is any wiser, the quest for transcendence ends in perplexity.

4.3   Caged Tigers: A Borgesian Theodicy

The dying Hunger Artist has no more wisdom to reveal than the execution machine that writes bloody nonsense on the prisoner's body. Taking the place of the delusional Hunger Artist's shriveled-up corpse, a panther delights the crowds with the unapologetic attractiveness of

---

[42] Bell-Villada 220.

[43] On the recurrent Borgesian conceit of "a magical object as a bane rather than a boon", see Kristal in Williamson (2013: 162).

vitality and youth. Borges's totemic animal clearly owes some of its DNA to Kafka's caged panther.[44] The tiger (along with its relatives, from the South American jaguar to the allegorical *lonza* of Dante's *Inferno*) is a privileged vehicle for the Borgesian epiphany—an experience defined by Fishburn as "equivocal, ambivalent, and ultimately elusive".[45] Revisiting the earlier story "The writing of the God" in the light of the later parable "*Inferno* I, 32", we find that it replicates the conjunction of magician/poet and tiger, while condensing the failed revelation motif into half a page. In both tales, the caged feline is at the nexus of a cosmic revelation withheld or forsaken, one that is "perhaps most devastatingly, of no consequence".[46] Tzinacán realizes that his fellow prisoner holds the key to the meaning of the universe, and that the message written on the animal's coat is intended for him alone. His renouncing the freedom and power granted by the revelation ("Let the mystery writ upon the jaguars die with me") anticipates the later parable, in which the pattern of revelation-and-renunciation is doubled in feline and human mirroring. The caged leopard's inability to comprehend the pain inflicted upon it replicates Dante's inability to understand the meaning of his own destiny and death in the cosmic scheme of things. Resorting to the same problematic teleology as Kafka's "Hunger Artist", God reveals to the leopard, in a dream, the purpose of its suffering: it is necessary so that Dante, having gazed at the animal, may create the allegorical *lonza* in his *Inferno*, which itself "*has its exact place in the weft of the universe. You suffer captivity, but you shall have given a word to the poem*" (*CF* 323). Years later, God reveals to a dying Dante "the secret purpose of his life and work" in a dream soon forgotten, which leaves him with the sense of having "received and lost an infinite thing". The twofold epiphany is withdrawn as soon as it is granted, leaving in its wake a sense of "obscure resignation" and ultimate opacity. "The machine of the world is exceedingly complex for the simplicity" of both man and beast.[47]

---

[44] Belitt 287; he also points out the intertext between "The Writing of the God" and Kafka's "Imperial message" (290).

[45] Fishburn (2015: 173).

[46] Ibid.

[47] See Slote's discussion of this parable in the context of Dantean allegory, especially 25–26.

The parables build up toward a revelation imminent yet unrealized, a quasi-Buddhist formula of the universe as suffering, of which the suffering animal is the cipher in its most basic form. But neither the suffering characters nor the reader will be granted the favor of an answer to the existential howl of rebellion.[48]

5   ELUSIVE MEANING: KAREN BLIXEN'S "A CONSOLATORY TALE"

Though contemporary, Borges and Karen Blixen (also known under the pseudonym Isak Dinesen) seem not to have read each other's work; yet there is much to gain by cross-reading their stories. Their literary reputations underwent strikingly parallel trajectories; they both achieved fame as world authors before being acclaimed in their native cultures.[49] They shared a disaffection for the realistic novel, preferring to craft metafictional, parable-like tales that exemplify the twentieth-century allegorical renaissance.[50] Nicknamed the Danish Scheherazade, Blixen thought of herself not as a writer, but as a storyteller.[51]

Blixen's enigmatic parable of renunciation, "A Consolatory Tale" (published in *Winter's Tales* in 1942), is a rewriting of the Buddha story blended with the adventures of Harun Al-Rashid and Eugène Sue's *Mysteries of Paris*. The tale is framed by a conversation in a Parisian café between a writer, Charles Despard, and the storyteller, Aeneas Snell, who once lived at the Persian court as a companion to the tale's hero, prince Nasrud-Din. Young, idealistic, "keen on progress and reform" (Blixen 1993: 296), an avid reader of both the *1001 Nights* and of Sue's socialist serial novel, Nasrud-Din resolved to imitate his heroes—Harun Al-Rashid and Prince Rudolph of Gerolstein—by disguising himself as a beggar and going incognito into the streets of Teheran to see for himself how his subjects lived. "He had studied the tales of the Arabian Nights,

---

[48]The parable opens on the caged leopard "howling in rebellion" (*CF* 323). Compare Borges's later assessment of the biblical Book of Job: "It is an enigmatic book because it deals with the enigma that is the universe, that we are, and because the author thinks by means of symbols, of metaphors" ("The Book of Job", in Aizenberg 275).

[49]Sollars and Jennings 224–225.

[50]Schwartz xxvi, also MacNiece 102 on parable as anti-realism.

[51]Landy 389–390.

and from this reading he fancied for himself the role of the Caliph Haroun of Bagdad" (296). Sue's Prince Rudolph, ruler of the fictional kingdom of Gerolstein, enjoyed dressing up as a working man and wandering into the slums of Paris to perform deeds of charity and justice, for which he was dubbed by Karl Marx "the German Haroun al-Rashid".[52] The young prince's decision to leave his palace, while motivated by political zeal, is thus densely mediated by literature. Nasrud-Din's quixotic propensity to act out literary situations is typical of Blixen's characters, and as Hannah Arendt pointed out, a weakness of Blixen herself: having made in the earlier part of her life the disastrous mistake of attempting to make reality live up to the story (especially her "absurd" marriage to her real love's twin brother), Blixen would later write stories ("The Dreamers", "The Poet", "The Immortal Story" all come to mind) about "the obvious lessons of her youthful follies, namely, about the 'sin' of making a story come true, of interfering with life according to a preconceived pattern".[53]

So it goes with Nasrud-Din. Like Siddharta's father king Suddodhana, Nasrud-Din's father has given orders to protect the prince, and to prevent him from seeing anything unpleasant. The ministers mobilize against his incognito outings: if they cannot prohibit them, they can turn them into fiction, paying off false "beggars" and "prostitutes" to delude the prince into thinking that all is well in Teheran. But things do not work out as planned. Nasrud-Din runs into his double, Fath, a beggar with an uncanny likeness to him, believed by the townspeople to be the prince in disguise.[54] The story climaxes in the dialogue between Fath and Nasrud-Din—between the prince disguised as a beggar and the beggar disguised as a prince disguised as a beggar. The prince's illusions unravel, as Fath reveals to him the harsh treatment his people endure. He learns that his soldiers attack poor people with impunity: Fath's own mother was killed in the marketplace, trampled by the horses of the prince's guard. Predictably, Nasrud-Din tries to assuage his guilt by giving gold

---

[52] In *The Holy Family* (1844). On the intertextual links between the adventures of Harun al-Rashid and the nineteenth century serial novel, see Jullien (2009: 25–70).

[53] Arendt (1968: 106–107). On the histrionic personalities of Blixen's characters and the recurring motif of Harun al-Rashid, see also Johanneson 29–30.

[54] Another intertextual layer here, the reference to "The Mock Caliph", a tale collected in Burton from the Calcutta II edition: Marzolph and Van Leeuwen I: 304–305.

to Fath; but Fath does not want gold. Instead, he dreams of rewriting history: he asks the prince to stage a repetition of the traumatic marketplace scene, where the horses would gently step over his body without hurting him. Both men want to make the story live up to reality: if the prince wants to act out a story in his life, the beggar wants to make life tell a different story. Inevitably, the encounter between prince and mendicant ends in an aporia, which Fath sums up in an aphorism: "the rich and the poor of this world are two locked caskets, each of which holds the key to the other" (Blixen 312).

The mystery persists; the beggar remains a beggar; the prince goes back to his palace: "I shall no more walk in my town in disguise" (312). Despite the expectations set up at the beginning of the tale (Harun al-Rashid or Prince Rudolph as models of good governance for Nasrud-Din to emulate) no political lesson is learned; no resolution is achieved, and despite the title, no consolation is offered.[55] Instead, the tale emphasizes the fictional nature of the king-and-beggar story over its moral or political message. The ending returns to the conversation between the two men in the Paris café. Readability is undermined by the frame tale's working at cross-purposes with the inset tale's moral. The conclusion comments on the artistic merits of the story, rather than its exemplarity: Charles Despard judges the story of Nasrud-Din "not a very good tale... but it has moments in it that might be worked up, and from which one might construct a fine tale" (313). Presumably Despard (the melancholy writer in need of a new theme) will "work up" the story told him by Aeneas Snell, perhaps indeed improving on it: the focus is on circulation, repetition, rewriting, rather than on content. Benjamin's diagnostic of Kafka's parables applies here as well: truth is sacrificed to transmissibility.[56] In Blixen's story-world as in Kafka's, everyone wants to be a courier.

Three riddle-like metaphors structure the tale, working simultaneously to invite metatextual interpretation and challenge it: life and death, man and woman, and finally rich and poor, are troped as locked caskets, suggesting a fourth, implicit, pair: the storyteller and his audience are two locked caskets, each of which holds the key to the other.[57] Blixen's

---

[55] See Wilkinson 85 on Blixen's stories' lack of closure.

[56] Benjamin 144; also Alter 59–60.

[57] On the narration's "parabolic quality", see Landy 405.

enigmatic story is constructed to defeat interpretation, in the manner of Kafka's parables which only tell us that "the incomprehensible is incomprehensible"; a statement echoed in her earlier story "The Dreamers": "It is not a bad thing in a tale that you understand only half of it".[58]

Time and again, in these stories, the wisdom at the end of the renunciatory quest eludes. The plasticity of renunciation narratives is what makes them mobile, adaptable and repeatable: however, this is achieved at the expense of the message's straightforwardness. Modern renunciation stories—whether Kafka's, Borges's, or Blixen's—are, like parables, a space of tension, where the pull toward a revelatory outcome is counteracted by an ironic force pushing (with perhaps Benjamin's "mighty paw") against an unambiguous answer. A story's enduring capacity to arouse the reader's "thoughtfulness", for Benjamin, lies in its mystery: "It is half the art of storytelling to keep a story free from explanation as one reproduces it".[59] A favorite storyteller's device to create this mystery is to displace the spotlight on the metatextual dimension, thus ensuring that the reader keeps shifting back and forth between "in reality" and "in parable". This tongue-in-cheek strategy is displayed in "Inferno I, 32", where Borges playfully rewrites the teleological argument in literal terms. The ethical issue at stake—the suffering of the innocent, with its immoral justification[60]—is posed and skewed, as the suffering is justified on ironically aesthetic grounds. The leopard suffers so that Dante may write him into his poem; similarly, and recursively, Dante suffers so that he may become a character in God's complex "poem" (the world). In parable (as Kafka would have it), God's justice is poetic; he too, like the writer, is in the business of creating plots by repetition and variation. The morphological intuition behind "The Plot"—which made teleological sense of the old gaucho's death at the hands of his godson by the necessity to repeat Caesar's murder (*CF* 307)—suggests a darkly ironic vision of universal history, which needs to repeat itself so that it can be put into story. By focusing on the telling—and retelling—of the tale, poetic justice substitutes for cosmogonic justification; the metaphysical gravity of the question is deflected into recursive self-reflection.

---

[58] Blixen (1991: 279).
[59] Benjamin "The Storyteller", 89.
[60] Lévinas 99, see Note 36.

CONCLUSION: RENUNCIATION STORIES AND WANDERING KINGS

In that way one can live. (*Life and Times of Michael K*)[1]

Ahora, la busca está condenada al fracaso. (*El oro de los tigres*)[2]

This book arose from a decision to follow an idea in movement. There was something intriguing about the Renunciation story that kept returning in various guises, in Borges's essays, poems, and stories. The story was simple enough—a king leaving his palace after an encounter with an ascetic—yet as Borges speculated that its various transformations revealed a foundational narrative principle, it seemed to lead down so many forking paths. It was identified with Buddhism, one of Borges's many intellectual interests: yet he appeared especially interested in the ways in which the story traveled beyond Buddhism, to the point where no one religion or culture could claim ownership to it. It circulated ubiquitously, and transformed itself almost beyond recognition. Politically, it set up a basic confrontation between power and powerlessness, but then flipped

---

[1]Coetzee 184.

[2]Today, the quest is doomed to failure. Translation mine. "Los cuatro ciclos", *OC* 2: 506.

© The Editor(s) (if applicable) and The Author(s),
under exclusive license to Springer Nature Switzerland AG 2019
D. Jullien, *Borges, Buddhism and World Literature*, Literatures
of the Americas, https://doi.org/10.1007/978-3-030-04717-7

the outcome because the powerless figure had the last word. Again this basic confrontation led down a multiplicity of possible political paths: reform, abdication or withdrawal being the main branches. The very plasticity of the Renunciation story and its metamorphic nature came at the expense of its outcome's political efficiency. As the king-and-ascetic pair morphed into a king-and-poet (or artist) pair, the story led down another path, the path of sacrificial aesthetics, with renunciation a key requirement of the creative process. Yet as portrayals of artists as renouncers—hermits, ascetics, cynics, or beggars—proliferated in narrative, the wisdom gained from their acts of abandonment lost its straightforwardness, either by self-sublimation into nothingness, a condition that affected so many modern artists real and fictional, or by casting doubt on the benefit to the renunciant. In this way, the Renunciation story showed a kinship with the parabolic predicament of modern literature: the storyteller still knew (and could retell) the story, but had lost confidence in the wisdom the story was meant to transmit.

This of course is not only Borgesian territory, and it makes the Renunciation story, so attractive to Borges, equally powerful beyond Borges. The "morphological" paradigm, which Borges borrowed from Goethe, is relevant initially as a Borgesian reading ethics and writing practice: but it can also be used productively as a strategy for reading other texts (attached to Borges either by traditional influence or the retrospective reading protocol described in "Kafka's Precursors") in a Borgesian web of interconnected narratives. Expanding on Christ's concluding image of Borges as "the hand that points" away from his own work and "through it to other writings",[3] the gamble of this book, therefore, was to take Borges at his word, so to speak, and attempt a reading of texts both by Borges and others, weaving in and out of Borges in pursuit of the protean Renunciation story.

* * *

One of the reading paths led from the Renunciation story to the parable, in particular the indecisive parables of modern literature. Post-transcendence, Benjamin felt, parables are bereft of any clear wisdom; they leave us stranded and groping in the dark. Still we seek the wisdom they seem to promise, even though we can no longer believe in it, even

---

[3]Christ 244.

though, in Benjamin's words, "only the products of its decay remain".[4] The Renunciation story, so compelling to modern storytellers, carries only "the imminence of a revelation", but one that never happens. Borgesian epiphanies fall short: "equivocal, ambivalent, and ultimately elusory, they both retain an element of the core meaning of the term, a vision of a transcendental, spiritual truth, while at the same time challenging its assumptions and undermining its significance".[5] There is no grand narrative in Borges's stories, where renunciation is viewed in the same dim light of skepticism—"insufficient... unceasing" like the light in the Library of Babel (*CF* 112)—that bathes all other creeds. If Buddhism appeals, it is largely because it is uniquely compatible with Borges's skeptical, agnostic worldview. Intellectual pursuits—the substance of so many of Borges's iconic stories—are similarly irresolute. "Pierre Menard", the first story of Borges's maturity, already suggested this quietly devastating denial of revelation: "There is no intellectual exercise that is not ultimately pointless" (*CF* 94).

The "exceedingly complex" machine of the world (*CF* 323) ensures that stories that narrate quests for understanding will never cease, and also never succeed. In laying out the archetypal stories that subsequent writers endlessly rewrite, transforming them, Borges's prose poem "Los cuatro ciclos" also points to the failure that attaches to modern quest narratives: today, the search fails. Intellectual revelations are foreclosed, a horizon always to be sought, never reached. The same uncertainty attaches to political action. The parable is an apposite vehicle for the failures of intellect, and also agency. A current of nihilism runs through modern renunciation stories: their austerity and minimalism signal a dissatisfaction with both philosophical and political certainties. For Borges, the act of abandonment that he found at the core of the Buddha legend, and that informed much of his writing, allowed a way of withdrawing into apolitical writing while also highlighting the perennial political conundrum. Beyond Borges, stories about renouncers, and more broadly the persistent dream of withdrawal from the polis that they convey, ultimately bring into sharper focus our current disaffection for the political.

* * *

---

[4]Benjamin 144.
[5]Fishburn (2015: 173).

Today the longing for an apolitical removal from the violence of power is perhaps as acute as ever. The political path branches off toward the pastoral mode,[6] a solution desired, but negated and thwarted: as parables fail us, as renunciation brings no wisdom, so pastoral is an option foreclosed to modern stories. Blixen's "Consolatory Tale" of a Persian prince leaving his palace remained politically inconclusive, with engagement and disengagement equally problematic. Looking to a more recent case, J. M. Coetzee's parables of renunciation in the face of anarchy exemplify this precarious, ambiguous "discourse of retreat".[7] It is tempting to cross-read Coetzee's mournful stories of abandonment against Borges's speculations on renunciation stories, not to engage in-depth with the already substantial scholarship on Coetzee, but simply to point to a harsher redrawing of the terms of the equation in the South African writer's fictions. Both *Life and Times of Michael K* and *Disgrace* problematize the recurrent dream of natural withdrawal, which is both dismissed as illusory and yet stubbornly clung to, as a fundamental, as perhaps the only consolation. Michael K, an innocent victim of a war in which he refuses to take sides, ascetic to the point of self-annihilation, plans to survive with a packet of seeds and a few spoonfuls of water after his farm is destroyed by soldiers. The book ends on this utterance of extreme dispossession: "In that way (he reflects), one can live".[8] On the other hand, David Lurie, the hapless anti-hero of the dark "anti-pastoral"[9] *Disgrace,* renounces his privileges as an educated white man in post-Apartheid South Africa, to take on the apparently meaningless task of incinerating dead dogs. These acts of abandonment tie the characters' fates to the canine etymology of the word "Cynic",[10] albeit without the authority that ancient stories granted Cynics over emperors, or ascetics over kings. David Lurie's sacrificial gestures (letting go of his favorite dog, renouncing to seek justice for the assault on his daughter, acquiescing to an animal-like existence), paradoxically align him with the vagrant Michael K, who is surely no kingly figure but always a "dumb dog", who begins life at the bottom and burrows even deeper by the end, holding fast to the barest form of survival and defining the good (enough) life

[6]On the pastoral mode, see Lavocat 12 and Alpers 6.
[7]Gifford 45.
[8]Coetzee (1985: 184).
[9]Lowry 12; also Barnard 386, 388–390.
[10]Rose 183–187; Wiegandt 130–134.

as merely being "out of all the camps at the same time".[11] Michael K's survival equipped with only a spoon, Lucy's grim determination to "start at ground level (...) like a dog",[12] yielding to her dispossession and degradation, Lurie's downward trajectory of "privilege eviscerating itself",[13] can be read in the context of modern renunciation stories, which afford their ascetic characters a correspondingly minimal, impoverished degree of wisdom.

* * *

The Renunciation story brings together the spiritual, political, and aesthetic aspects of asceticism, opening up a space of creative give-and-take. In doing so, it may well provide the only satisfying answer to the perplexities of metaphysics: in non-dogmatic story form. It is not that Borges turned to writing fictions because he reached an impasse in his mystical quest, because "essayistic truths" fell short of his "serious metaphysical anxieties".[14] This fundamentally flawed reading fails to acknowledge that the aesthetic purpose is no less "serious" for a writer of fictions. It is important to take Borges's aesthetic solutions to metaphysical problems seriously: not by elevating metaphysics as the "real" object of Borges's creative labors—downplaying the poetic in favor of the philosophical—but by elevating fiction as a serious response to metaphysical anxiety. As Beatriz Sarlo put it, "The Borges literary machine fictionalizes these questions, producing a *mise en forme* of theoretical and philosophical problems".[15] Borges claimed for himself the poet's place: "I am neither a thinker nor a moralist, but simply a man of letters who turns his own perplexities and that respected system of perplexities we call philosophy into the forms of literature".[16] Among these "forms" is the seminal and multifaceted legend of the Great Renunciation. Stories do not claim to solve the questions: more importantly, they rehearse

[11]Coetzee (1985: 28, 182).

[12]Coetzee (1999: 205).

[13]Rose 187. He also makes the connection with Borges's "Dialogues of Ascetic and King" (186).

[14]Flynn 17.

[15]Sarlo 5; also Griffin in Williamson (2013: 5–6), Dove (2007: 170) and Balderston (1996: 202).

[16]Borges's Foreword to Christ xv. The Foreword to *In Praise of Darkness* restates this ironic allegiance to "the perplexities which not without some arrogance are called metaphysics" (*CG* 331).

and re-enact them in multiple reincarnations of patterns and variations. The lack of an answer, as Blixen (and Arendt) knew, can be made into a good story. Stories are an ancient form of non-response to metaphysical questions, which is perhaps why they are the vehicle of choice for many of the writers discussed in these pages.[17] The questions raised by the Renunciation story are appropriately reworked in extratemporal variations on the ancient archetype. Today, it is possible to revisit Borges's archetypal model of narrative, along with Structuralists' theories of plots as re-enactment of archetypal actions,[18] in light of the work of cognitive narratologists in recent years. Archetypes, in this perspective, can said to be "universal" not in any vague essentialist sense, but as fundamental forms of human mental life: it would be a productive line of inquiry to analyze Borgesian morphologies in terms of David Herman's "narrative microdesigns" or Patrick Colm Hogan's "universal narrative prototypes", for example.[19] This would be the starting point for another book.

* * *

To conclude this journey, we turn once again to the twilight story, "Blue Tigers". Alexander Craigie's act of abandonment—renouncing his intellectual sovereignty, academic confidence, and imperial sense of superiority—fails to grant him the expected wisdom. The reliable protocol of transmission appears broken. Of the blind beggar, we know only that Craigie did not see him disappear after he accepted the burden of the stones. Appropriately for a deathbed story,[20] "Blue Tigers" weaves a dense web of intertextual allusions: Kipling's Indian tales, Conrad's *Heart of Darkness*, the *1001 Nights* story where the blind beggar asks the caliph to slap him,[21] and of course Borges's own "Zahir" (*CF* 242) are all layered in the narrative. The reworking of key intratextual motifs from "The Zahir" is especially striking. The coin/tiger reversibility is common to both stories—Craigie too has "looked upon the tiger" and fears losing

[17]On Blixen's choice of an archaic form and the repetitiveness of her plots, see Cavarero 129–134 and Landy 399.

[18]See for example Britton 608–610.

[19]Hogan 134–138 and Herman 27.

[20]Shortly before his death Borges decided to include "Blue Tigers" (which had appeared in 1978 in *La Nación* under the title "El milagro perdido") in a new and final collection bearing the title of one of its four stories, *Shakespeare's Memory*. On the compositional history of the last collection of tales see *OCP* II: 1444–1446.

[21]Galland/Mack 727.

his mind like the Narrator in the "Zahir" (*CF* 247)—while Craigie's fevered probability calculations with the stones (501–502) rewrite the game of *truco* which lures "Borges" into the bar in "The Zahir" (*CF* 244), troping the narrative of human destinies as the infinite combinations of a finite number of recurring patterns.[22] The intertextual density seems crafted to illustrate the resigned epilogue of "The Immortal": "*As the end approaches... there are no longer any images from memory—there are only words.* Words, words, words taken out of place and mutilated, words from other men—those were the alms left him by the hours and the centuries" (*CF* 195). The morphological recombination of narrative forms derived from the renunciation archetype ensures that the story renounces any claim to individuality.

What makes this story so powerful is precisely that it combines radical impersonality with metatextual potential. Borges's late story is about stories. A story about a blue tiger—unverified, anonymous, multiple—sends Craigie on a quest where, guided and misled in equal measure by the villagers' stories (their various fictional sightings of the blue tiger) he finds the blue stones, coin-like in appearance (497), whose untraceability, multiplication, and dissemination relate them to the uncountable stories from the *1001 Nights.* That they are handed to the blind beggar (Homer?) suggests that the blue stones are also coins given in payment of a story: the accepted loss of ownership makes "Blue Tigers" a parable of narrative circulation.[23]

The archetypal king-and-ascetic trope applies metatextually to the Borgesian view of world literature: like the king leaving his palace to wander out into the world and beg from strangers, a writer leaves behind the comfort but also the limitations of national tradition to "beg" sustenance from other languages and literary cultures. No longer tied to one tradition, his kingdom becomes the world, his birthright, the universe (*SNF* 427). In this model, canonicity is of little significance. Borges consistently pairs canonical examples with non-canonical ones in the light of eternity. "Whoever goes down to a river goes down to the Ganges. / Whoever looks at an hourglass sees the dissolution of an empire. / Whoever plays with a dagger foretells the death of Caesar", he writes

---

[22]Corroborated by the early poem "Truco", *SP* 12–13.

[23]Also note Dove's reading of the coin trope in connection with an aesthetics of metaphor as differential repetition (Dove 2007: 175).

in a late poem.[24] Julius Caesar's death is the same as the gaucho's (CF 307). An idiosyncratic feeling-in-death experience in a run-down suburb of Buenos Aires is juxtaposed to Berkeley's and Schopenhauer's grand narratives (SNF 324–326). Borges equalizes the "kings" and the "beggars" among stories, ensuring that no character, no destiny, no story is more important than another, that they morph and circulate without concern for place, time or hegemony.[25] Nor is the Borgesian model concerned with the destruction of palaces. Rather, it resonates with contemporary strategies of globalized reading, concurrently cross-reading texts from various times, places and traditions. Neither interested in drawing up a list of canonical works, nor in consigning them to the dustbins of literary history, the Borgesian strategy makes comparison "prevail over the codification of the canonical".[26] As the literary king wanders across the world, having renounced his sovereignty, national and otherwise, he leaves the center behind, radiating centrifugally toward far-flung traditions[27] (the Scandinavian rewriting of an Indian archetype) but also, conversely, rejoining the central story from distant margins (the Englishwoman writing back to the Barbarian defending Ravenna). Not coincidentally, the king and the ascetic, the center and the periphery, but also the reader and the writer, meet in the morphological labyrinth of ramifying stories. Like Pascal's sphere, which also ushered morphological conjectures on history as "various intonations of a few metaphors" (SNF 353), the Borgesian story of world literature is one in which the center is everywhere, the periphery nowhere.

[24]"Happiness", The Limit, SP 440.

[25]In Dove's words, literary history for Borges is not about the canon: instead, it is "an archive of possibilities for deviation, transformation and actualization of unrealized possibilities" (Dove 2014: 44).

[26]Cooppan 186.

[27]Dimock (2001: 178 and 2007: 1).

WORKS CITED

WORKS BY JORGE LUIS BORGES, COLLABORATIONS AND INTERVIEWS

Note: Since this study is crosscultural and may be of interest not exclusively to Hispanists, texts by Borges are quoted in English translation whenever possible, relying primarily on the various Penguin editions, and supplemented when necessary by the original Spanish editions and occasionally French-language scholarly editions.

OC: *Obras completas*. Buenos Aires: Emecé, 1989–2007, 4 volumes.
BB: *La biblioteca de Babel*. Buenos Aires: Emecé, 2000.
TC: *Textos cautivos*. Barcelona: Tusquets, 1990.
CF: *Collected Fictions*, tr. Andrew Hurley. New York: Penguin Books, 1998.
SNF: *Selected Non Fictions*, ed. Eliot Weinberger. New York: Penguin Books, 1999.
SP: *Selected Poems*, ed. Alexander Coleman. New York: Penguin Books, 1999.
AE: "An Autobiographical Essay", in *The Aleph and Other Stories, 1933–1969*. New York: Dutton, 1970.
CV: *This Craft of Verse*, ed. Calin-Andrei Mihailescu. Cambridge: Harvard University Press, 2000.
S: *The Sonnets*, eds. Stephen Kessler and Suzanne J. Levine. New York: Penguin Classics, 2010.

© The Editor(s) (if applicable) and The Author(s), under exclusive license to Springer Nature Switzerland AG 2019
D. Jullien, *Borges, Buddhism and World Literature*, Literatures of the Americas, https://doi.org/10.1007/978-3-030-04717-7

OM: On Mysticism, eds. María Kodama and Suzanne J. Levine. New York: Penguin Books, 2010.

PN: Poems of the Night, ed. Efraín Kristal. New York: Penguin Books, 2010.

SN: Seven Nights, tr. Eliot Weinberger, intro. Alastair Reid. New Directions, 2009.

OW: On Writing, ed. S.J. Levine. New York: Penguin Books, 2010.

PA: A Personal Anthology, ed. Anthony Kerrigan. New York: Grove, 1967.

OCP: Œuvres complètes, ed. J.-P. Bernès. Paris: Gallimard, Bibliothèque de la Pléiade: 1999–2010, 2 volumes.

HI: Histoire de l'infamie – Histoire de l'Eternité, Postface by Roger Caillois. Paris: Société Générale d'Editions, 1971.

QB: Borges, J.L., and Alicia Jurado, *¿Qué Es El Budismo?* Buenos Aires: Editorial Columba, 1976.

Borges, J.L., Alicia Jurado, and Pedro L. Barcia. *Borges, El Budismo y yo*. Buenos Aires: Academia Argentina de Letras, 2011.

———. "Kipling's Colonialism and Style", tr. Anthony Tudisco, *Pulpsmith* 1:4 (Winter 1981): 32–34.

———, Cristina Parodi, and Iván Almeida. "Borges en diálogo sobre el Budismo", *Variaciones Borges* 20 (2005): 101–124.

———, and Jacques Chancel. *Jorge Luis Borges: Radioscopie*. Paris: Editions du Rocher, 1999.

———, and Osvaldo Ferrari. *Libro de diálogos*. Buenos Aires: Sudamericana, 1986.

OTHER LITERARY WORKS

Arnold, Edwin. *The Light of Asia, or, The Great Renunciation*. [1879] Chicago: Rand-McNally, 1890.

Aśvaghoṣa and Patrick Olivelle. *Life of the Buddha*. New York: New York University Press, 2008.

Blixen, Karen [Isak Dinesen]. *Seven Gothic Tales*. New York: Vintage, 1991.

———. *Winter's Tales*. New York: Vintage, 1993.

Burton, Richard Francis. *A Plain and Literal Translation of the Book of the Thousand Nights and a Night (with Introduction, Terminal Essay and Supplemental Nights)*. Private Subscription by the Kama Shastra Society [London], 16 volumes, 1885–1888.

Cicero. *Tusculan Disputations*, tr. J.E. King. *Cicero in Twenty Eight Volumes: Vol. 18*. Loeb Classical Library. Cambridge, MA: Harvard University Press, 1971.

Coetzee, J.M. *Life and Times of Michael K*. London and New York: Penguin Books, 1985.

————. *Disgrace*. New York: Viking, 1999.

Confucius. *Analects*, tr. by A. Charles Muller, 1990, online: http://www.acmuller.net/con-dao/analects.html.

Chrysostom, Dio. *Discourses*. Harvard: Loeb Classical Library, 1932.

de Balzac, H. *The Unknown Masterpiece*, tr. Richard Howard, *The New York Review Books*, 2001.

de Voragine, Jacobus. *The Golden Legend*, tr. W.G. Ryan. Princeton: Princeton University Press, 2012.

Laertius, Diogenes. *Lives of Eminent Philosophers*, tr. R.D. Hicks. Cambridge: Harvard University Press [1925], 1972.

Euripides. *The Phoenician Women, in Orestes and Other Plays*, tr. Philip Vellacott. London: Penguin Books, 1972.

Flaubert, Gustave. *La Tentation de saint Antoine*. Paris: Garnier frères, 1968.

————. *Correspondance*. Paris: Conard, 1910–1954, 13 volumes.

————. *The Temptation of Saint Anthony*, tr. Lafcadio Hearn, intro. Michel Foucault. New York: Modern Library, 2001.

Galland, Antoine (translator). *Arabian Nights Entertainments* [Galland version], ed. Robert L. Mack. New York: Oxford University Press, 1995.

————. *Les Mille et une nuits, Contes arabes*, eds. Aboubakr Chraïbi and Jean-Paul Sermain. Paris: Garnier-Flammarion, 2004, 3 volumes.

Hearn, Lafcadio. *A Japanese Miscellany*. Boston: Little-Brown, 1901.

Herodotus. *The Histories*, tr. Aubrey de Sélincourt. London: Penguin Books, 2003.

Hugo, Victor. *William Shakespeare*, in *Œuvres complètes*. Paris: Club français du livre, 1967–1969, volume 12.

Joyce. *A Portrait of the Artist as a Young Man* [1916]. London: Granada, 1977.

Kafka, Franz. *The Complete Stories*. New York: Schocken Books, 1971.

————. *Parables and Paradoxes*. New York: Schocken Books, 1972.

Kipling, Rudyard. *Kim*, intro. Edward Said. London: Penguin Classics, 1989.

————. *The Jungle Books*, ed. Kaori Nagai. London: Penguin Classics, 2013.

Mahfouz, Naguib. *Arabian Nights and Days*, tr. Denys Johnson-Davies. London: Doubleday, 1995.

Mun-yol, Yi. *The Poet*, tr. Chong-Wha Chung and Brother Anthony of Taizé. London: Harvill Press, 1995.

Plutarch. *Plutarch's Lives*, tr. J. Langhorne and W. Langhorne. London: Tegg, 1848.

Poe, E.A. "The Oval Portrait", in *Complete Stories and Poems of Edgar Allan Poe*. New York: Doubleday, 1966.

Sarma, Visnu. *Panchatantra*, tr. Chandra Rajan. Penguin Classics, 2006.

Schwartz, Howard. *Tales of Wisdom: 100 Modern Parables*. New York: Crescent Books [1976], 1991.

Schwob, Marcel. *Imaginary Lives*, tr. Lorimer Hammond. New York: Boni and Liveright, 1924.

——. *Le Voyage à Samoa: Lettres à Marguerite Moreno*. Paris: Ombres, 1990.

——. *La Croisade des enfants*. Toulouse: Petite Bibliothèque Ombres, 1992.

Tacitus, Cornelius. *The Annals: The Reigns of Tiberius, Claudius and Nero*, tr. J.C. Yardley. Oxford: Oxford University Press, 2008.

The Animals' Lawsuit Against Humanity, tr. Seyyed Hossein Nasr. Louisville, KY: Fons Vitae, 2005.

The Case of the Animals Versus Man Before the King of the Jinn: A Translation from the Epistles of the Brethren of Purity, tr. Lenn E. Goodman and Richard McGregor. Oxford University Press, 2009.

The George Sand—Gustave Flaubert Letters, tr. Aimee L. McKenzie. London: Duckworth and Co., 1922.

The Letters of Gustave Flaubert: 1857–1880, selected and ed. Francis Steegmuller. Harvard University Press, 1982.

Wilde, Oscar. *The Happy Prince and Other Stories*. London: David Nutt, 1910. Project Gutenberg etext: http://www.gutenberg.org/dirs/etext97/hpaot10h.htm.

Yourcenar, Marguerite. *En pèlerin et en étranger. Essais*. Paris: Gallimard, 1989.

——. *Oriental Tales*, tr. Alberto Manguel. New York: Noonday Press, 1990.

Zola, Emile. *The Masterpiece*, tr. Roger Pearson. Oxford: Oxford University Press, 1993.

CRITICAL WORKS ON BORGES

Aizenberg, Edna. *The Aleph Weaver: Biblica, Kabbalistic and Judaic Elements in Borges*. Potomac, MD: Scripta Humanistica, 1984.

Alazraki, Jaime. *Borges and the Kabbalah: And Other Essays on His Fiction and Poetry*. Cambridge: Cambridge University Press, 1988.

——. "Borges's Modernism and the New Critical Idiom", in Edna Aizenberg (ed.), *Borges and His Successors: The Borgesian Impact on Literature and the Arts*. Columbia and London: Missouri University Press, 1990: 99–108.

Almond, Ian. "Borges the Post-orientalist: Images of Islam from the Edge of the West", *Modern Fiction Studies* 50:2 (2004): 435–459.

Apostol, Gina. "Borges, Politics and the Postcolonial", *Los Angeles Review of Books*, August 18, 2013: lareviewofbooks.org/article/borges-politics-and-the-postcolonial/.

Balderston, Daniel. "Octuple Allusion in Borges's *Inquisiciones*", in K. David Jackson (ed.), *Transformations of Literary Language in Latin American Literature: From Machado de Assis to the Vanguards*. Austin: Abaporu Press, 1987: 75–78.

————. "Borges, Averroes, Aristotle: The Poetics of Poetics", *Hispania: A Journal Devoted to the Teaching of Spanish and Portuguese* 79:2 (1996): 201–207.

————. "Borges: The Argentine Writer and the 'Western' Tradition", in Evelyn Fishburn (ed.), *Borges and Europe Revisited*. University of London, Institute of Latin American Studies, 1998: 37–48.

Balderston, Daniel, Gastón Gallo, and Nicolás Helft. *Borges: una enciclopedia*. Barcelona: Norma, 1999.

Barili, Amelia. "Borges, Buddhism, and Cognitive Science", *Religion East and West* 9 (October 2009): 47–58.

Belitt, Ben. "The Enigmatic Predicament: Some Parables of Kafka and Borges", *Prose for Borges, TriQuarterly* 25 (1972): 269–293.

Bell-Villada, Gene H. *Borges and His Fiction: A Guide to His Mind and Art*. Austin: University of Texas Press, 1999.

Berveiller, Michel. *Le Cosmopolitisme de Jorge Luis Borges*. Paris: Didier, 1973.

Bosteels, Bruno. "Beggars' Banquet: For a Critique of the Political Economy of the Sign in Borges", *Variaciones Borges* 29 (2010): 3–52.

Bossart, William H. *Borges and Philosophy: Self, Time, and Metaphysics*. New York: P. Lang, 2003.

Britton, R.K. "History, Myth and Archetype in Borges's View of Argentina", *Modern Language Review* 74:3 (July 1979): 607–616.

Caillois, Roger. "The Masked Writer", *Review: Literature and Arts of the Americas* 7:8 (1973): 29–32.

Christ, Ronald. *The Narrow Act: Borges' Art of Allusion*. New York: Lumen Books, 1995.

Dove, Patrick. "Metaphor and Image in Borges's 'El Zahir'", *The Romanic Review* 98:2–3 (March–May 2007): 169–187.

————. "Aesthetics, Politics and Event: Borges's 'El fin', the Argentine Tradition and Death", *The New Centennial Review* 14:1 (Spring 2014): 25–46.

Fiddian, Robin. *Postcolonial Borges: Argument and Artistry*. Oxford: Oxford University Press, 2017.

Fishburn, Evelyn. "Jewish, Christian and Gnostic Themes", in Edwin Williamson (ed.), *The Cambridge Companion to Jorge Luis Borges*. Cambridge: Cambridge University Press, 2013: 56–67.

————. *Hidden Pleasures in Borges's Fiction*. Pittsburgh: Borges Center, University of Pittsburgh, 2015.

Flynn, Annette U. *The Quest for God in the Work of Borges*. London: Continuum, 2009.

Friedman, Mary Lusky. *The Emperor's Kites: A Morphology of Borges' Tales*. Durham: Duke University Press, 1987.

García, Carlos. "Borges y Kafka", *Revista De Occidente* 301 (2006): 33–43.

García, Jacobo. "Marcel Schwob y la re-ingeniería creativa de Borges", *Rinconete*, Centro Virtual Cervantes, 10 junio 2011, online.

Genette, Gérard. *Palimpsests: Literature in the Second Degree*. Lincoln: University of Nebraska Press, 1997.

Golieth, Catherine. "Yourcenar et Borges: Conditions et effet de dichroïsme de la réécriture", *Bulletin de la Société Internationale d'Etudes Yourcenariennes* 20 (1999): 173–187.

Griffin, Clive. "Philosophy and Fiction", in Edwin Williamson (ed.), *The Cambridge Companion to Jorge Luis Borges*. Cambridge: Cambridge University Press, 2013: 5–15.

Irby, James E. *The Structure of the Stories of Jorge Luis Borges*, PhD dissertation, University of Michigan (Ann Arbor, MI: University Microfilms, 1962).

Jullien, Dominique. "Biography of an Immortal", *Comparative Literature* 47:2 (Spring 1995): 136–159.

———. "In Praise of Mistranslation: The Melancholy Cosmopolitanism of Jorge Luis Borges", *Romanic Review* 98: 2–3 (March–May 2007): 205–223.

Levine, Suzanne Jill. "A Universal Tradition: The Fictional Biography", *Review: Literature and Arts of the Americas* 7:8 (1973): 24–28.

Kleingut de Abner, Berta. *Marcel Schwob, Jorge Luis Borges: marginalidad y trascendencia*. San Juan: EFFHA, 2006.

Kodama, María. "Oriental Influences in Borges' Poetry: The Nature of the Haiku and Western Literature", in Carlos Cortínez (ed.), *Borges the Poet*. Fayetteville: University of Arkansas Press, 1986: 170–181.

Kristal, Efraín. *Invisible Work: Borges and Translation*. Nashville: Vanderbilt University Press, 2002.

———. "The Book of Sand and Shakespeare's Memory", in Edwin Williamson (ed.), *The Cambridge Companion to Jorge Luis Borges*. Cambridge: Cambridge University Press, 2013: 160–171.

Lafon, Michel. *Borges ou la réécriture*. Paris: Seuil, 1990.

Message, Vincent. "Les deux rois et les deux labyrinthes: J.L. Borges, J. Joyce et l'idée d'efficacité romanesque", *Littérature* 153 (March 2009): 3–18.

Nichanian, Marc. "On the Archive, III: The Secret; or, Borges at Yale" (tr. Gil Anidjar), *Boundary 2, an International Journal of Literature & Culture* 40:3 (2013): 1–38.

Novillo-Corvalán, Patricia. "Joyce's and Borges's Afterlives of Shakespeare", *Comparative Literature* 60:3 (Summer 2008): 207–227.

O'Sullivan, Gerry. "Intertextuality in Borges and Foucault", in Edna Aizenberg (ed.), *Borges and His Successors: The Borgesian Impact on Literature and the Arts*. Columbia: University of Missouri Press, 1990: 109–121.

Paoli, Roberto. "Borges y Schopenhauer", *Revista de Crítica Literaria Latinoamericana* 12:24 (1986): 173–208.

Rodríguez Monegal, Emir. *Jorge Luis Borges, a Literary Biography.* New York: Dutton, 1978.

Roger, Sarah. "Finding Franz Kafka in the Works of Jorge Luis Borges", *Oxford German Studies* 43:2 (2014): 144–155.

Rose, Arthur. *Literary Cynics: Borges, Beckett, Coetzee.* London: Bloomsbury, 2017.

Rowlandson, William. "Confronting the Shadow: The Hero's Journey in Borges' 'El Etnógrafo'", *Journal of Romance Studies* 12:2 (Summer 2012): 17–32.

Salha, Agathe. "Entre histoire et fiction: les Vies imaginaires dans les œuvres de Walter Pater, Marcel Schwob et Jorge Luis Borges", *La Réserve* [En ligne], November 30, 2015.

San Francisco, Alexander. "Los papeles de 'El Buddha legendario', pretextos de *Qué es el Budismo*", *Variaciones Borges* 38 (July 2014): 147–156.

Sarlo, Beatriz. *Jorge Luis Borges: A Writer on the Edge.* London and New York: Verso, 1993.

Siskind, Mariano. "El cosmopolitismo como problema político: Borges y el desafío de la modernidad", *Variaciones Borges* 24 (2007): 75–92.

Slavuski, Victoria. "The Old Man and the City", *Times Literary Supplement,* August 20, 1999: 10–12.

Slote, Sam. "Stuck in Translation: Borges and Beckett on Dante", *Journal of Beckett Studies* 19:1 (2010): 15–28.

Sturrock, John. *Paper Tigers: The Ideal Fictions of Jorges Luis Borges.* Oxford: Clarendon Press, 1977.

Toro, Alfonso de. "La 'literatura menor', concepción borgesiana del 'Oriente' y el juego de las referencias. Algunos problemas de nuevas tendencias en la investigación de la obra de Borges", *Iberoromania* 53 (2001): 68–110.

Waisman, Sergio. *Borges and Translation: The Irreverence of the Periphery.* Lewisburg: Bucknell University Press, 2005.

Wheelock, Carter. *The Mythmaker: A Study of Motif and Symbol in the Short Stories of Jorge Luis Borges.* Austin: University of Texas Press, 1969.

Williamson, Edwin. *Borges: A Life.* New York: Viking, 2004.

———. "Borges Against Perón: A Contextual Approach to 'El Fin'", *Romanic Review* 98:2–3 (March–May 2007): 275–296.

———. (ed.). *The Cambridge Companion to Jorge Luis Borges.* Cambridge: Cambridge University Press, 2013.

Woodall, James. *Borges, a Life.* New York: Basic Books, 1996.

Younes, Ebtehal. "Jorge Luis Borges y el patrimonio filosófico oriental", *Variaciones Borges* 2 (1996): 87–99.

Zonana, V.G. "*De viris pessimis:* Biografías imaginarias de Marcel Schwob, Jorge Luis Borges y Juan Rodolfo Wilcock", *Rilce* 16:3 (2000): 673–690.

OTHER CRITICAL WORKS

Allamand, Carole. *Marguerite Yourcenar: une écriture en mal de mère*. Paris: Imago, 2004.

Almond, Philip C. "The Buddha of Christendom: A Review of the Legend of Barlaam and Josaphat", *Religious Studies* 23 (1987): 391–406.

——. *The British Discovery of Buddhism*. Cambridge: Cambridge University Press, 1988.

Alpers, Paul. *The Singer of the Eglogues: A Study of Virgilian Pastoral*. Berkeley: University of California Press, 1976.

Alter, Robert. *Defenses of the Imagination: Jewish Writers and Modern Historical Crisis*. Philadelphia: Jewish Publication Society of America, 1977.

Arendt, Hannah. *Men in Dark Times*. New York: Harcourt, Brace & World, 1968.

——. *The Human Condition*. Chicago: Chicago University Press, 1998.

——. *Between Past and Future*. New York: Penguin Books, 2006.

Auerbach, Erich. "Philology and *Weltliteratur*", in Theo D'Haen et al. (eds.), *World Literature: A Reader*. London and New York: Routledge, 2012: 65–73.

Ballaster, Ros. *Fabulous Orients: Fictions of the East in England 1662–1785*. Oxford University Press, 2005a.

—— (ed.). *Fables of the East, Selected Tales 1662–1785*. Oxford University Press, 2005b.

Barbier, Catherine. *Etude Sur Marguerite Yourcenar, Les Nouvelles Orientales*. Paris: Ellipses, 1998.

Barnard, Rita. "Coetzee's Country Ways", *Interventions: International Journal of Postcolonial Studies* 4:3 (2002): 384–394.

Baumann, Martin. "The Transplantation of Buddhism to Germany: Processive Modes and Strategies of Adaptation", *Method & Theory in the Study of Religion* 6:1 (1994): 35–61.

Bem, Jeanne. *Désir et savoir dans l'œuvre de Flaubert*. Paris and Lausanne: Payot, 1979.

Benjamin, Walter. *Illuminations*, ed. Hannah Arendt, tr. Harry Zohn. New York: Schocken, 1968.

Berg, Christian (ed.). *Retours à Marcel Schwob: d'un siècle à l'autre, 1905–2005*. Rennes: Presses Universitaires de Rennes, 2007.

Bernheimer, Charles. "'Être la matière!': Origin and Difference in Flaubert's *La Tentation de saint Antoine*", *Novel: A Forum on Fiction* 10:1 (1976): 65–78.

Berman, Antoine. "Goethe: traduction et littérature mondiale", in *L'Epreuve de l'étranger: culture et traduction dans l'Allemagne romantique*. Paris: Gallimard, 1984: 87–110.

Bollème, Geneviève. *Extraits de la Correspondance: ou, Préface à la vie d'écrivain*. Paris: Seuil, 1963.

Brooks, Peter. "Flaubert: The Tragic Historian", *New York Review of Books*, March 9, 2017: 24–26.

Caracciolo, Peter. "Buddhist Teaching Stories and Their Influence on Conrad, Wells, and Kipling: The Reception of the Jataka and Allied Genres in Victorian Culture", *Conradian* 11:1 (1986): 24–34.

Cavarero, Adriana. *Relating Narratives: Storytelling and Selfhood*. London: Routledge, 2000.

Cheng, François. *Vide et plein, le langage pictural chinois*. Paris: Seuil, 1991.

Clausen, Christopher. "Sir Edwin Arnold's *The Light of Asia* and Its Reception", *Literature East and West* 17 (1973): 174–191.

———. "Victorian Buddhism and the Origins of Comparative Religion." *Religion* 5:1 (1975): 1–15.

Cooppan, Vilashini. "World Literature and Global Theory: Comparative Literature for the New Millennium", in Theo D'Haen et al. (eds.), *World Literature: A Reader*. London and New York: Routledge, 2012: 176–197.

Cornille, Jean-Louis. "Contes sans nouvelles: Marcel Schwob et Cie", in Christian Berg and Yves Vadé (eds.), *Marcel Schwob d'hier et d'aujourd'hui*. Seyssel: Champ Vallon, 2002: 298–319.

Crossan, J.D. *Raid on the Articulate: Comic Eschatology in Jesus and Borges*. Eugene, OR: Wipf and Stock, 1976.

———. *The Dark Interval: Toward a Theology of Story*. Farmington, MN: Polebridge Press, 1988.

Damrosch, David. *What Is World Literature?* Princeton: Princeton University Press, 2003.

Degner, Uta. "What Kafka Learned from Flaubert: 'Absent-Minded Window Gazing' and 'The Judgment'", in Stanley Corngold and Ruth V. Gross (eds.), *Kafka for the 21st Century*. Rochester, NY: Camden House, 2011: 75–88.

Deleuze, Gilles, and Félix Guattari. *Kafka: pour une littérature mineure*. Paris: Minuit, 1975.

Dimock, Wai Chee. "Literature for the Planet", *PMLA* 116:1 (January 2001): 173–188.

Dimock, Wai Chee, and Lawrence Buell (eds.). *Shades of the Planet: American Literature as World Literature*. Princeton: Princeton University Press, 2007.

Dyrberg, Torben Bech. *Foucault on the Politics of Parrhesia*. Houndsmill: Palgrave Macmillan, Pivot, 2014.

Engelstein, Stefani. *Anxious Anatomy: The Conception of the Human Form in Literary and Naturalist Discourse*. Albany: SUNY Press, 2008.

Fabre, Bruno. "Vies imaginaires de philosophes: Marcel Schwob lecteur de Diogène Laërce", *Revue de Littérature Comparée* 317 (January–March) 2006: 37–52.

———. *L'Art de la biographie dans* Vies imaginaires *de Marcel Schwob*. Paris: Champion, 2010.

Filaire, Marc-Jean. "'Comment Wang-Fô fut sauvé,' Récit d'une disparition et disparition du récit", *Bulletin de la Société Internationale d'Etudes Yourcenariennes* 24 (2003): 59–74.

Foucault, Michel. *The Order of Things: An Archaeology of the Human Sciences.* New York: Vintage, 1970.

———. "La bibliothèque fantastique", in Raymonde Debray-Genette et al. (eds.), *Travail de Flaubert.* Paris: Seuil, 1983: 103–123.

———. *The Courage of Truth (The Government of Self and Others II): Lectures at the Collège De France, 1983–1984,* ed. Frédéric Gros, tr. Graham Burchell. New York: Palgrave Macmillan, Picador, 2012.

France, Peter. *Hermits: The Insights of Solitude.* New York: St Martin's Press, 1996.

Fulton, Bruce. "Yi Mun-Yol", in Joshua S. Mostow et al. (eds.), *The Columbia Companion to Modern East Asian Literature.* New York: Columbia University Press, 2003.

Funk, Robert. *Funk on Parables: Collected Essays,* ed. Bernard Brandon Scott. Santa Rosa, CA: Polebridge Press, 2006.

Geddes, Jennifer L. *Kafka's Ethics of Interpretation: Between Tyranny and Despair.* Evanston, IL: Northwestern University Press, 2016.

Gerhardt, Mia. *The Art of Story-Telling: A Literary Study of the Thousand and One Nights.* Leiden: E.J. Brill, 1963.

Gerould, Gordon Hall. "The Hermit and the Saint", *PMLA* 20:3 (1905): 529–545.

Ghazoul, Ferial. *Nocturnal Poetics: The Arabian Nights in Comparative Context.* Cairo, Egypt: American University in Cairo Press, 1996.

Gifford, Terry. *Pastoral.* London and New York: Routledge, 1999.

Glaudes, Pierre (éd.). *Léon Bloy au tournant du siècle.* Toulouse: Presses Universitaires du Mirail, 1992.

Goethe. *Essays on Art and Literature, Collected Works,* ed. John Gearey. Princeton University Press, 1986, volume 3.

———. "The Metamorphosis of Plants", in Douglas Miller (ed.), *The Collected Works, Volume 12: Scientific Studies.* Princeton University Press, 1995.

Grassi, Marie-Claire. "Le Taoïsme dans 'Comment Wang-Fô fut sauvé'", *Bulletin de la Société Internationale d'Etudes Yourcenariennes* 24 (2003): 75–87.

Green, Martin. *Dreams of Adventure, Deeds of Empire.* New York: Basic Books, 1979.

Grosrichard, Alain. *The Sultan's Court: European Fantasies of the East,* tr. Liz Heron. London and New York: Verso, 1998.

Guillén, Claudio. "*Weltliteratur*", in Theo D'Haen et al. (eds.), *World Literature: A Reader.* London and New York: Routledge, 2012: 142–149.

Halley, Achmy. *Marguerite Yourcenar en poésie: Archéologie d'un silence.* Amsterdam: Rodopi, 2005.

Harpham, Geoffrey Galt. *The Ascetic Imperative in Culture and Criticism.* Chicago: University Chicago Press, 1987.

———. "Asceticism and the Compensations of Art", in Vincent L. Wimbush and Richard Valantasis (eds.), *Asceticism.* New York: Oxford University Press, 1995: 357–368.

Hayashi, Osamu. "L'imaginaire orientaliste chez Marguerite Yourcenar", in Georges Fréris and Rémy Poignault (eds.), *Marguerite Yourcenar écrivain du XIXe siècle?* Clermont-Ferrand: SIEY, 2004: 241–249.

Heller-Roazen, Daniel. *Dark Tongues: The Art of Rogues and Riddlers.* New York: Zone Books, 2013.

Herman, David. *Story Logic: Problems and Possibilities of Narrative.* Lincoln and London: University of Nebraska Press, 2002.

Hershinow, David. "Diogenes the Cynic and Shakespeare's Bitter Fool: The Politics and Aesthetics of Free Speech", *Criticism* 56:4 (2014): 807–835.

Hogan, Patrick Colm. *Cognitive Science, Literature and the Arts.* New York and London: Routledge, 2003.

Inaga, Shigemi. "The Painter Who Disappeared in the Novel: Images of an Oriental Artist in European Literature", in Martin Heusser et al. (eds.), *Text and Visuality.* Amsterdam: Rodopi, 1999: 117–127.

Irwin, Robert. "The Arabic Beast Fable", *Journal of the Warburg and Courtauld Institutes* 55 (1992): 36–50.

———. "Political Thought in *The Thousand and One Nights*", *Marvels and Tales* 18: 2 (2004): 246–257.

Jackson, Michael. *The Politics of Storytelling: Variations on a Theme by Hannah Arendt.* Copenhagen: Museum Tusculanum Press, 2013.

Johanneson, Eric. "The Mask in Isak Dinesen's Tales", in Olga Pelensky (ed.), *Isak Dinesen: Critical Views.* Athens: Ohio University Press, 1993: 29–37.

Jouanno, Corinne. "*Barlaam et Joasaph*: une aventure spirituelle en forme de roman d'amour", in *Essais sur la perfection: le héros et le saint*, éd. Robert Baudry, *Pris-MA, Recherches sur la littérature d'imagination au Moyen Age II,* tome XVI, 1, 31, janvier–juin 2000: 61–76.

Julien, Anne-Yvonne. *Anne-Yvonne Julien Commente* Nouvelles Orientales *de Marguerite Yourcenar.* Paris: Gallimard, 2006.

Jullien, Dominique. *Les Amoureux de Schéhérazade: variations modernes sur les 1001 Nuits.* Geneva: Droz, 2009.

———. "Vie imaginaire de Léonard de Vinci", *Bulletin des Etudes valéryennes* 72–73 (November 1996): 263–275.

———. "Le 'ventre' de Paris: pour une pathologie du symbolisme dans *L'Oeuvre* d'Emile Zola", *French Forum*, September 1992: 281–299.

Kalouche, Fouad. "The Cynic Way of Living", *Ancient Philosophy* 23 (2003): 181–194.

Koh, Helen. *The Columbia Companion to Modern East Asian literature*, eds. Bruce Fulton et al. New York: Columbia University Press, 2003: 644–645.

Kris, Ernst, and Otto Kurz. *Legend, Myth and Magic in the the Image of the Artist: A Historical Experiment*, Preface by E.H. Gombrich. New Haven and London: Yale University Press, 1979.

Krul, Wessel. "Adolf Loos and the Doric order", in Evert Peeters et al. (eds.), *Beyond Pleasure: Cultures of Modern Asceticism*. New York: Berghahn Books, 2011: 123–143.

Landy, Marcia. "Anecdote as Destiny: Isak Dinesen and the Storyteller", *The Massachusetts Review* 19:2 (Summer 1978): 389–406.

Laude, Patrick. "La Connaissance orientale et le féminin chez Marguerite Yourcenar", *Symposium: A Quarterly Journal in Modern Literatures* 60:2 (2006): 81–92.

Lavocat, Françoise. *Arcadies malheureuses, aux origines du roman moderne*. Paris: Champion, 1998.

Leclerc, Yvan. "'Madame Bovary, c'est moi', formule apocryphe", *Centre Flaubert*, mis en ligne Février 2014.

Lefkowitz, Jeremy B. "Aesop and Animal Fable", in Gordon Lindsay Campbell (ed.), *The Oxford Handbook of Animals in Classical Thought and Life*. Oxford University Press, 2014: 1–23.

Lescart, Alain. "Marguerite Yourcenar aux prises avec le taoïsme dans le conte 'Comment Wang-Fô fut sauvé'", *Bulletin de la Société Internationale d'Etudes Yourcenariennes* 25 (2004): 21–30.

Lévinas, Emmanuel. "Useless Suffering", in *Entre-Nous: Thinking-of-the-Other*. Columbia University Press, 1998.

Lhermitte, Agnès. *Palimpseste et merveilleux dans l'œuvre de Marcel Schwob*. Paris: Champion, 2002.

London, Jennifer. "How to Do Things with Fables: Ibn Al-Muqaffa's Frank Speech in Stories from *Kalila wa Dimna*", *History of Political Thought* XXIX:2 (Summer 2008): 189–212.

Lopez, Donald S., and Peggy McCracken. *In Search of the Christian Buddha: How an Asian Sage Became a Medieval Saint*. New York: Norton, 2014.

Lowry, Elizabeth. "Like a Dog", *London Review of Books* 21:20 (1999): 12–14.

Lussier, Mark. *Romantic Dharma: The Emergence of Buddhism into Nineteenth-Century Europe*. New York: Palgrave Macmillan, 2011.

MacNiece, Louis. *Varieties of Parable*. London and New York: Cambridge University Press, 1965.

Makdisi, Saree. *Romantic Imperialism: Universal Empire and the Culture of Modernity*. Cambridge: Cambridge University Press, 1998.

Manguel, Alberto. *A History of Reading*. New York: Penguin Books, 1997.

Marin, Louis. "Essai d'analyse structurale d'un récit-parabole: Mt 13, 1–23", in C. Chabrol and L. Marin (eds.), *Le Récit évangélique*. Paris: Aubier, 1974: 93–192.

Marzolph, Ulrich, and Richard van Leeuwen. *Arabian Nights Encyclopedia*. Santa Barbara: ABC-Clio, 2004, 2 volumes.

Melchionne, Kevin. "Why Artists Starve", *Philosophy and Literature* 31:1 (2007): 142–148.

Menéndez Pidal, Ramón. *El condenado por desconfiado, de Tirso de Molina* (Discurso leído ante la Real Academia Española en la recepción pública de D. Ramón Menéndez Pidal), Madrid: Tello, 1902: 5–56 (Digitized by the Internet Archive 2013: http://archive.org/details/discursoelconden00menn).

Milanetti, Giorgio. "Why Would a King Become an Ascetic? A Few Political Answers from Hindi Medieval Literature", in Paola M. Rossi and Cinzia Pieruccini (eds.), *Kings and Ascetics in Indian Classical Literature*. Milano: Cisalpino, 2009: 267–295.

Mitchell, Breon. "Kafka and the Hunger Artists", in Alan Udoff (ed.), *Kafka and the Contemporary Critical Performance: Centenary Readings*. Bloomington: Indiana University Press, 1987: 236–255.

Molendijk, Arie L. *Friedrich Max Müller and the Sacred Books of the East*. Oxford: Oxford University Press, 2016.

Naithani, Sadana. "The Teacher and the Taught: Structures and Meanings in the *Arabian Nights* and the *Panchatantra*", *Marvels and Tales* 18:2 (2004): 272–285.

Naveh, Gila Safran. *Biblical Parables and Their Modern Re-creations: from "Apples of Gold in Silver Settings" to "Imperial Messages"*. Albany: SUNY Press, 2000.

Neubauer, John. "Morphological Poetics?", *Style* 22:2 (Summer 1988): 263–274.

———. "Organic Form in Romantic Theory: The Case of Goethe's Morphology", in Larry H. Peer (ed.), *Romanticism Across the Disciplines*. Lanham, New York, and Oxford: University Press of America, 1998: 207–230.

Neiland, Mary. *'Les tentations de saint Antoine' and Flaubert's fiction: A Creative Dynamic*. Amsterdam: Rodopi, 2001.

Norris, Margot. "Sadism and Masochism in Two Kafka Stories: 'In Der Strafkolonie' and 'Ein Hungerkünstler'", *Modern Language Notes* 93:3 (1978): 430–447.

Ogden, Thomas H. "Kafka, Borges, and the Creation of Consciousness, Part I: Kafka—Dark Ironies of the 'Gift' of Consciousness", *The Psychoanalytic Quarterly* (2009): 343–367.

Olivelle, Patrick. *Ascetics and Brahmins: Studies in Ideologies and Institutions.* London: Anthem Press, 2011.

Perrin, Norman. "The Parables of Jesus as Parables, as Metaphors, and as Aesthetic Objects: A Review Article", *The Journal of Religion* 47:4 (October 1967): 340–346.

Pierce, Jerry B. *Poverty, Heresy, and the Apocalypse: The Order of Apostles and Social Change in Medieval Italy, 1260–1307.* London: Continuum, 2012.

Pizer, John D. *The Idea of World Literature: History and Pedagogical Practice.* Baton Rouge: Louisiana State University Press, 2006.

Pizzagalli, A.M. "Influssi buddhistica nella leggenda di Alessandro", *Rendiconti dell'Istituto Lombardo* 76 (1942–1943): 154–160.

Politzer, Heinz. *Franz Kafka: Parable and Paradox.* Ithaca, NY: Cornell University Press, 1962.

Posnock, Ross. *Renunciation: Acts of Abandonment by Writers, Philosophers, and Artists.* Cambridge: Harvard University Press, 2016.

Propp, Vladimir. *Morphologie du conte.* Paris: Points Seuil, 1970.

Rabaté, Dominique. "Vies imaginaires et vies minuscules: Marcel Schwob et le romanesque sans roman", in Christian Berg and Yves Vadé (eds.), *Marcel Schwob d'hier et d'aujourd'hui.* Seyssel: Champ Vallon, 2002: 177–191.

Reid, Martine. *Flaubert correspondant.* Paris: SEDES, 1995.

Rhys Davids, T.W. *The Questions of King Milinda,* in F.M. Müller (ed.), *The Sacred Books of the East.* Oxford: Clarendon Press, 1879, volumes 35–36.

———. "Buddhism and Christianity", *The International Quarterly* 7 (1903): 1–13.

Riotto, Maurizio. "Yi Mun-yol", in Alba Amoia and Bettina L. Knapp (eds.), *Multicultural Writers Since 1945: An A-to-Z Guide.* Westport, CT: Greenwood, 2004: 534–535.

Rolleston, James. "Purification unto Death: 'A Hunger Artist' As Allegory of Modernism". In Richard T. Gray (ed.), *Approaches to Teaching Kafka's Short Fiction.* New York: Modern Language Association of America, 1995: 135–142.

Ryan, Christopher. *Schopenhauer's Philosophy of Religion: The Death of God and the Oriental Renaissance.* Leuven: Peeters, 2010.

Scholes, Robert. *Structuralism in Literature: An Introduction.* New Haven: Yale University Press, 1974.

Séginger, Gisèle. *Naissance et métamorphoses d'un écrivain: Flaubert et "Les Tentations de saint Antoine".* Paris: Champion, 1997.

Shklovsky, Victor. "Art as Technique", in Lee T. Lemon and Marion J. Reis, *Russian Formalist Criticism: Four Essays.* Lincoln: University Nebraska Press, 1965.

Sloterdijk, Peter. *Critique of Cynical Reason.* Minneapolis: University Minnesota Press, 1987.

Sollars, Michael, and Arbolina L. Jennings. *The Facts on File Companion to the World Novel: 1900 to the Present.* New York: Facts on File, 2008.

Song, Anna. "'Comment Wang-Fô fut sauvé' et la peinture chinoise", *Société Internationale d'Etudes Yourcenariennes* 16 (1996): 85–92.

Sontag, Susan. *Essays of the 1960s and 1970s.* New York: Library of America, 2013.

Spineto, Natale. "The Notion of Archetype in Eliade's Writings", *Religion* 38:4 (2008): 366–374.

Stead, Evanghélia. "Marcel Schwob, l'homme aux livres", in Christian Berg (ed.), *Retours à Marcel Schwob, d'un siècle à l'autre, 1905–2005.* Rennes: Presses Universitaires de Rennes, 2007: 29–49.

Steiner, George. "A Footnote to *Weltliteratur*", in *Le Mythe d'Etiemble: Hommage, Etudes et recherches.* Paris: Didier, 1979: 261–269.

Strich, Fritz. *Goethe and World Literature.* London: Routledge & K. Paul, 1949.

Suh, Ji-moon. "Yi Mun-yol", in Joshua S. Mostow et al. (eds.), *The Columbia Companion to Modern East Asian Literature.* New York: Columbia University Press, 2003: 727–730.

Suleiman, Susan Rubin. *Authoritarian Fictions: The Ideological Novel as a Literary Genre.* Princeton University Press, [1983] 1993.

Terneuil, Alexandre. "L'Art du portrait chez Marguerite Yourcenar ou Portrait de l'homme en artiste sage", *Bulletin de la Société Internationale d'Etudes Yourcenariennes* 29 (2008): 47–64.

Thiher, Allen. *Franz Kafka, a Study of the Short Fiction.* Boston: Twayne, 1990.

Toporov, V.N. "A Few Remarks on Propp's Morphology of the Folktale", in Victor Erlich et al. (eds.), *Russian Formalism: A Retrospective Glance: A Festschrift in Honor of Victor Erlich.* New Haven: Yale Center for International and Area Studies, 1985.

Valantasis, Richard. "A Theory of the Social Function of Asceticism", in Vincent L. Wimbush and Richard Valantasis (eds.), *Asceticism.* New York: Oxford University Press, 1995: 544–552.

Vázquez de Parga, Maria José. "Lecture de Jorge Luis Borges et de Marguerite Yourcenar à travers le miroir", in Rémy Poignault and Blanca Arancibia (eds.), *Lectures transversales de Marguerite Yourcenar.* Tours: Société Internationale d'Etudes Yourcenariennes, 1997: 99–110.

Viegnes, Michel. "Marcel Schwob: une écriture plurielle", in Christian Berg and Yves Vadé (eds.), *Marcel Schwob d'hier et d'aujourd'hui.* Seyssel: Champ Vallon, 2002: 242–256.

Vigée Lebrun, Elisabeth. *Souvenirs*, ed. Claudine Hermann. Paris: Editions des Femmes, 1984, 2 volumes.

Wiegandt, Kai. "J.M. Coetzee's 'Dog-Man' and the Cynicism of *Disgrace*", *Anglia* 131:1 (2013): 121–140.

Wilkinson, Lynn R. "Hannah Arendt on Isak Dinesen: Between Storytelling and Theory", *Comparative Literature* 56:1 (Winter 2004): 77–98.

Wilson, Angus. "*Kim* and the Stories", in *Kipling*. "Bloom's Modern Critical Views". Chelsea House 1987: 23–33.

Wilson, Edmund. "The Kipling That Nobody Read", in Andrew Rutherford (ed.), *Kipling's Mind and Art: Selected Critical Essays*. Stanford University Press, 1966: 17–69.

Wimbush, Vincent L., and Richard Valantasis (eds.). *Asceticism*. New York: Oxford University Press, 1995.

Wright, Brooks. *Interpreter of Buddhism to the West: Sir Edwin Arnold*. New York: Bookman Associates, 1957.

Yongjia, Liang. "Renouncers in Chinese World: Reconsidering Gentry and 'Local Elites'", *Asia Research Institute Working Paper Series* 143 (September 2010): 3–18.

Yourcenar, Marguerite, and Matthieu Galey. *With Open Eyes: Conversations with Matthieu Galey*. Boston: Beacon Press, 1984.

Zhang, Yinde. "Perspectives orientalistes: Yourcenar et le taoïsme", in Jean Bessière (ed.), *Perspectives Comparatistes*. Paris: Champion, 1999: 313–335.

Zhu, Jing. "Art and Daoism in 'How Wang-Fo Was Saved'", *Theory and Practice in Language Studies* 6:6 (June 2016): 1279–1283.

INDEX

© The Editor(s) (if applicable) and The Author(s),
under exclusive license to Springer Nature Switzerland AG 2019
D. Jullien, *Borges, Buddhism and World Literature*, Literatures
of the Americas, https://doi.org/10.1007/978-3-030-04717-7

L
La Fontaine, Jean de, 28
Lalitavistara, xiii
Levine, Suzanne Jill, 20, 61, 62
Light of Asia, The. See Arnold, Edwin

M
Mahfouz, Naguib, 38
Majjhima-nikaya, xiii
Manguel, Alberto, xxii
Martin, Agnes, 77
Martín Fierro, 15
Metrocles, 65
Milinda (King) or Menander, xii, xiv,
  24, 27, 38
Milinda Pañha, xiii–xv, 6, 27
Morphology, xx–xxi, xxii–xxiii, xxiv,
  2–4, 6–9, 11, 14, 15, 24, 27, 46,
  48, 49, 97, 100, 104–106
Müller, Günther, 7, 8
Müller, Max, xiv–xvi
Mun-yol, Yi, xxiv, 48, 52, 72–74

N
Nagasena, xii, 27
Napoleon, 11
Naveh, Gila S., 86
Nirvana, xv, xvi

O
Oriental, Orientalism, Orientalist, xiv–
  xv, xvii, xix, xxi–xxii, 27, 31, 36,
  37, 42, 55, 57, 68–70, 72

P
Panchatantra, 27–29
Parrhesia, xxiv, 26, 31, 36–38
Pascal, Blaise, 10, 106

Pastoral, 102
Perón, Juan Domingo, 18–19
Petronius, 63, 64
Plutarch, 26
Politzer, Heinz, 85, 86
Posnock, Ross, xxiv, 77–79
Propp, Vladimir, xxiii, 7–9, 49
Proust, Marcel, 16, 17, 65

R
Renunciation, xxv, 2–3, 4–5, 12,
  13, 14, 16, 18–24, 24, 25, 27,
  30, 35, 38–39, 40–42, 44, 48,
  52, 56, 57, 60, 65, 66, 70, 71,
  72–73, 75, 77–81, 83–84, 89, 90,
  92–94, 97, 99–105
Rhys Davids, T.W., xiii–xvi, xix, xx
Rose, Arthur, xxiv, 102
Russian Formalism, 9

S
Schariar, Shahryar, Shahriyar, 28, 29,
  31–38
Scheherazade or Shahrazad, 21, 28,
  29, 31–34, 38, 63, 94
Schopenhauer, Arthur, xvii, xviii, 7,
  61, 106
Schwob, Marcel, xxiv, xxv, 48, 52,
  60–67, 69
Shakespeare, William, xviii, 3, 4, 31,
  79–81, 91
Shklovsky, Victor, 9
Siddharta, xii, 2, 4, 5, 25, 26, 30, 31,
  71, 95
Sloterdijk, Peter, 24, 26, 60
Spengler, Oswald, 6–8, 14
Strich, Fritz, 11
Structuralism, xxiii, 9, 84, 88, 104
Suddodhana, 95
Suzuki, Daisetsu Teitaro, xv

CPSIA information can be obtained
at www.ICGtesting.com
Printed in the USA
LVHW082016080119
603171LV00012B/244/P